David Adam was born in Alnwick, Northumberland. He was Vicar of Danby on the North Yorkshire Moors for over 20 years, where he discovered the gift for writing prayers in the Celtic pattern. His first book of these, *The Edge of Glory*, achieved immediate popularity. He has since published several collections of prayers and meditations based on the Celtic tradition and the lives of the Celtic saints. His books have been translated into various languages, including Finnish and German, and have appeared in American editions. Many of his prayers have now been set to music. After 13 years as Vicar of Holy Island, where he had taken many retreats and regularly taught school groups on prayer, David moved to Waren Mill in Northumberland from where he continues his work and writing.

THE WONDER OF
THE BEYOND

David Adam

Illustrations by Monica Capoferri

First published in Great Britain in 2011

Society for Promoting Christian Knowledge
36 Causton Street
London SW1P 4ST
www.spckpublishing.co.uk

British Library Cataloguing-in-Publication Data
A catalogue record for this book is available from the British Library

ISBN 978–0–281–06330–7

1 3 5 7 9 10 8 6 4 2

Typeset by Graphicraft Ltd, Hong Kong
Printed in Great Britain by J F Print Ltd., Sparkford, Somerset

Produced on paper from sustainable forests

To Denise and all who have opened my eyes to wonder

A man who has lost his sense of wonder is a man dead.
(William of Thierry, 1085–1148)

Contents

Introduction

This is not an autobiography but reveals points in my life when I have been nudged to open my eyes and my heart, to move in new directions and into deeper awareness of what is all about me. In this way it is not a book primarily about me but about awe and wonder and only then my reaction to them. It is written in the belief that we belong to a world that is far greater than we can even imagine. It is written with the plea that we open our eyes, our ears and our hearts to the wonder and the mystery that is all around us.

At home every now and again I would be told, 'There is no one like you.' This was usually followed by the words 'Thank God'. So I was never sure whether it was an act of praise or a plea to conform. However, I have grown to believe more and more that each one of us is a special person, a one-off, and that we are all unique. No one else sees quite like we see, or hears quite like we hear. We can be recognized by our fingerprints, our eye print, our hair, our saliva or samples of our DNA. Even if we are an identical twin there is still no one truly like us. Our experiences are different from each other's. So we each have our own story to tell, our own song to sing and our own love to share. If we do not do these things no one else can do it for us. If we try and have the same story as someone else then we become play-actors and cease to be ourselves. This is what the Bible calls hypocrisy.

Yet there is another side to this for every story has something that is familiar to the rest of us. There is much common ground and it is often other people's story or song, other people's joys and sorrows that help us to open our eyes. Those who see deeply help us to see more clearly; those who teach us to love draw out love from us. Often the task of opening our eyes is the work of poets and artists and visionaries in the sciences as much as that of the Church. But above all it is left to our loved ones to draw us out and help us to see we are loved for who we are and who we could be. There is nothing like the wonder of being loved for drawing out our potential and helping us to be someone in our own right. It is true that 'love changes everything' and, in the words of St Paul, 'without love I am nothing'. Love draws us out from being a no thing to being a living and loving person and that is awesome, it is wonder-full.

Today many people walk around in a haze feeling quite lost. They do not know who they are or what they alone can do. Such people often hide behind drink and drugs or in hyper-activity, and some hide in a religion that cocoons them from facing reality. Before the Church can call them to deny themselves it needs to teach them how to be themselves. No one can give themselves until they have a self to give. We need to learn how to be, and to encourage others to be also. Quite often we will only find this self, this power to be, when someone has turned to us in love and has accepted us as a person in our own right. We are given the potential for change after we are accepted for who we are in love. This fills our lives with awe and wonder and in its turn helps us to reach out in confidence and with a love of our own.

There are many times when we need to seek the gate between the 'two worlds' to discover they are not two but one, that earth and heaven are one. The division is only in our own mind. We have created the fences and barriers. There is not another distant world where God dwells. God is here, God is with us, and above all God is. This is the world in which God is with you and that God gives to you every moment of your life. Why do you look for another? Are you not delighted with God's gift? Why look to eternity when you dwell in it in the now? The greatest judgement may be that we have spurned and spoiled what God has given to us – dare such people be let loose in another world? If you seek to discover the heights and depths of this world, you will discover wonder upon wonder and the mystery of the great Other who is God. The simple request of God to us is 'Be opened' (Mark 7.34). The poet William Blake in 'A Memorable Fancy' said, 'If the doors of the perception were cleansed everything would appear to man as it is, infinite.'

The prophets of the Old Testament were often called seers; it was their ability to look into the depths of what was around them that made them able to see the beyond. We often fail to get to the reality that is about us for we have not looked deep enough or stayed there long enough. Join me in a journey to be more open to the world around us, to enter into a wonder-full world. I hope that on this journey you will discover that:

1 Every single thing is unique and full of wonder.
2 Each thing is a subject in its own right.
3 Every thing within creation has a potential to create awe.
4 Every single moment is in eternity. We are explorers of a world without frontiers.
5 You are in God and God is in you.

It is no use saying 'I know all this'; you have to experience it each day, as the wonder of the day unfolds. It needs to be your own personal experience. Heed these words by D. H. Lawrence:

> Now the great and fatal fruit of our civilisation, which is a civilisation based on knowledge, and hostile to experience, is boredom. All our wonderful education and learning is producing a grand sum total of boredom. They are bored because they experience nothing. And they experience nothing because the wonder has gone out of them. And when wonder has gone out of a man he is dead. He is henceforth only an insect.

When all comes to all, the most precious element in life is wonder. Love is a great emotion, and power is power. But both love and power are based on wonder. Love without wonder is a sensational affair, and power without wonder is mere force and compulsion. The one universal element in consciousness which is fundamental to life is the element of wonder . . . the sense of wonder. That is our sixth sense. And it is the natural religious sense.

> (D. H. Lawrence, 'Hymns in a Man's Life'
> in Anthony Beal (ed.), *D. H. Lawrence: Selected
> Literary Criticism*, Heinemann, 1982, pp. 7–8)

It is not enough to have our experience vicariously; we must cultivate our own sense of wonder and awe. It is sad to sit and watch adventures on the television unless we have adventures of our own. So, I invite you to join with me to walk the frontiers of life and the world. Let us realize that we still walk in communion with the mystery that is all around us. Let us seek to renew our sense of awe and of holiness. Let us open our eyes to see that the sacred is not confined to the Church – it is within all of creation, for God created it all.

At the end of each chapter I will leave you with a quotation to challenge your thinking and an exercise to help you practise being open to the beyond in our midst. You may like to start by making this your daily prayer:

> Lord, Creator of all,
> Open my eyes to your presence:
> Open my ears to your call:
> Open my heart to your love.

The wonder of the beyond

There was a time, when meadow, grove, and stream,
The earth, and every common sight,
To me did seem
Apparelled in celestial light,
The glory and the freshness of a dream..
(William Wordsworth, 'Intimations of
Immortality', stanza 1, 1807)

My father said it was fortunate that he put his hand through the mechanical saw; he lost two fingers and almost severed a third. Even though he had been attached to his fingers, he reckoned this was an action that changed his life for the better. The result was a time in hospital and the sack from his job for not using the saw properly! This was in the 1930s when the unemployment figures had reached three million. He felt he could not stay at home in Dundee and be a further drain on his parents. He took to the roads to find work. As it was the beginning of summer he went north; most people were going southwards. He worked or begged for food. He lived as a 'clootie hoosie', that is he had a makeshift tent using an old piece of waterproofed cloth (cloot) which he made into a house (a tent or hoose).

One day he begged a meal from the monks at Fort Augustus at the west end of Loch Ness. He planned to make his way to Fort William but it was not to be. Coming in the other direction was a group of travellers and they all camped together for the night. Among the travellers he was attracted to a young English woman and for them both it seemed to be love at first sight. My father's direction was changed: he would re-travel the road he had come along keeping pace with 'Bonnie Mary'. The very next night at Drumnadrochit they decided their journey through life should be together. They let the travellers leave without them. Taking three days to travel 15 miles, and sleeping in their clootie hoosie at night, they arrived at Inverness and there they were married. They had no money, no home, no possessions and no real prospects. But they had love, the beauty of the landscape and youth on their side.

Idylls rarely last forever. They had a glorious romantic summer though they often went hungry. By the late autumn there was no more casual work, no fruit left in the hedgerows, no secure shelter in their makeshift tent. The first frosts and snow of the coming winter were signs of trouble ahead. By now Mary was expecting her first child. The Highlands were no longer an option for them. They made their journey south, first to Dundee and then on to Northumberland and to Alnwick, my mother's home town. By now both were undernourished. For a short while they were cared for by Mary's parents. Her father, my grandfather, was the town's lamplighter and his income was very small. He was affectionately known as 'Oompah'. He was part of the local Salvation Army band, and played a brass instrument but it was said all you could ever hear from it was 'Oompah, Oompah'. Fortunately Grandma was a good cook and could rustle up a meal with a few bones, an onion and some potato. However my mother would lose her first children, twins, due to malnutrition and the poverty in which they lived. This was far from uncommon in the 1930s when so many were unemployed and living below the breadline.

Soon they were given a house to rent next to my grandparents. It was in a cobbled courtyard of eight houses and backed onto the Correction House. Eight households shared the one water pump in the yard and an earth closet not far from it! This was truly a medieval set-up. The house had two bedrooms though the second room was very small and had no windows. Into this house I was born. Next door were my grandparents, three uncles and an aunt who was only six years older than I.

Fortunately by the time I entered the world in 1936 my father was employed as a labourer and bringing in a small wage. Now and again my father said, 'You do not know how lucky you are to be here.' This was in relation to his losing his fingers and meeting up with my mother. Without these events I would not have existed. If you look at our universe and the emptiness of so much space, we are all truly lucky to exist. At this moment in time ours is the only planet we know of that is conducive to life as we know it. We should give thanks and rejoice in the wonder of our being. You may like to stop for a while and do just that.

When war was declared, the 'good fortune of losing fingers' was at work again. My father was counted not fit for the forces. But, as he could drive, he was given a job with the NAAFI. He would drive around the camps and airfields delivering various foodstuffs and cigarettes. This meant while so many families 'lost' the man of the house to the war my father was still at home. It also meant that I travelled with him all over north Northumberland, calling at airfields and being welcomed by men who were missing their own children. One of my early memories is being lifted into a Spitfire to see what it was like. I also remember visiting prisoner-of-war camps and thinking how nice many of these people were.

Wherever we went my father encouraged me to use my eyes. To look and take in what was around me. He would point out places of interest or something moving in a field. I can remember trips in the blackout over the moors with the road shining like a silver ribbon and seemingly going on forever. I felt I was part of a radiant and mysterious world, a world where there were adventures galore for those with eyes to see. It is a pity if we lose this awareness as we grow.

My parents loved walking and often at weekends or in the evenings walked by the River Aln near the imposing Alnwick Castle. In one of the first photographs of me, I am sitting with my father on top of a carved lion which is on top of the lion bridge over the River Aln. It was a precarious position with a steep drop to the river on one side and the old A1 road on the other side. Health and Safety would have gone mad! From an early age I was discovering that life is to be adventured and that we cannot remain forever in a safe place. To extend our selves or our vision is often a risky business but can be a great joy.

We would watch the rabbits at play and the fish jumping in the river; sometimes we saw a red squirrel or a fox and occasionally a few deer. We did not seek to name everything we saw but we enjoyed the sighting of a new bird or creature. I discovered that every day brought something new to see or experience: no day is a repeat of the day that has gone before.

Because our house was small it encouraged us to go out into the surrounding countryside. I lived in a land of open fields, moorland and beaches: a land of castles, of history, of heroes, saints and story. By the time I went to school, I had begun to learn the stories of the area in which I lived and to notice the changes in seasons and scenery. I was learning to 'read' what was around me. I was beginning to discover sensitivity and a wonder towards all of life from flower and tree to all of the animals. I can still remember going with a jam jar to catch some minnows or sticklebacks. I was successful and watched these creatures swimming frantically around the jar. I thought the bright blue circles around the stickleback's eyes were very special. I admired the fish and regarded their beauty but I decided I could not keep them confined like this. I walked back to the river and put them back where I found them. This was all part of a growing sense of wonder and respect towards what was around me.

Another time I can remember standing beneath an ash tree in the spring and being awestruck at its beauty. I stood for a long time staring into its greening branches, just enjoying this strange connection with another piece of creation. Somehow I was aware that it existed in its own right, that it had its own being. Just as later in life I refused to try and capture the glory of sunsets with my camera, I discovered I could not find words to explain my awareness of the ash tree. When two friends came by and wanted to know what I was looking at they could not understand what I saw. They said it was 'only a tree'. They could not see the extra-ordinariness in it being what it was. I was learning to love the world, its beauty and the glory within it. Everything seemed full of life, a radiant world that forever offered something new.

The world I lived in was full of the mystery of existence. The wonder is that I was, I am, here to enjoy it. I exist and the tree exists, the lark in the sky, the frog in the pond and the bird in its nest all exist. The sun, the moon and the stars all exist in their own right and are different from each other. My eyes and my heart had opened to what Wittgenstein called 'existential wonder'. I wanted to look further, see deeper, to enjoy mysteries. I never thought of possessing these things, only to enjoy them and to give my attention to them. Later when I read Emily Dickinson's poem I felt how well it expressed how I felt in those times:

> But were it told me – Today –
> That I might have the sky
> For mine – I tell you that my Heart
> Would split, for size of me –
>
> The Meadows – mine –
> The Mountains – mine –
> All Forests – Stintless Stars –
> As much of Noon as I could take
> Between my finite eyes –

> The Motions of the Dipping Birds –
> The Morning's Amber Road –
> For Mine – to look at when I liked –
> The News would strike me dead.
> (Emily Dickinson, *The Complete Poems*,
> Faber & Faber, 1970, p. 155)

On another occasion I went on a Sunday-school outing with the Baptist church. It was all the more special because we travelled by courtesy of the local coal man on his coal cart. It was wonderful to sit behind the horse as we travelled through the parkland at Alnwick. We passed the fifteenth-century gate tower of Alnwick Abbey on our way to Hulne Abbey. We looked at the 'trysting tree' between the two abbeys where it is thought the monks from the abbeys met. We travelled alongside the River Aln until we stopped at the Lady's Well to look at it, if not to drop a pin in it and make a wish. At last we arrived at Hulne Abbey to have our games and a picnic. This group of majestic ruins with its high surrounding wall and an ancient yew caught my imagination. There were stone carvings of a couple of monks at what was the main gate. Here the first Carmelite monastery in England was founded in the thirteenth century. It was said the abbey was built on this site because the hill opposite looked like Mount Carmel. I can still remember enjoying the races and the picnic but more than this I was overawed by the wonderful ruins and the fact that white-robed monks had walked here. I thought of how peaceful and beautiful it must have been to live there. I would return to the abbey many a Sunday afternoon in my teens. The beauty and the stillness of the parks as well as the abbey became part of my birthright. It was not only a wonder-full world, it was also my Holy Land. It was while attending the Baptist Sunday school that I sang for the first time:

> God, who made the earth,
> The air, the sky, the sea,

Who gave the light its birth,
Careth for me.

God, who made the grass,
The flow'r, the fruit, the tree,
The day and night to pass,
Careth for me.

God, who made the sun,
The moon, the stars, is He
Who, when life's clouds come on,
Careth for me.

God, who made all things,
On earth, in air, in sea,
Who if I lean on Him,
Will care for me.
(Sarah Betts Rhodes, 1829–1904)

Hymns would, and still do, make a great impact on my awareness. Singing and affirming at the same time seems to enter deeper into my being. Though, I must admit I learnt my twelve times tables the same way. The hymns and songs that I sang at the Salvation Army and at the Baptist church not only moved me but also entered my memory as resources to call on in times of dryness or doubt as well as to express joy and awe. In many ways the simple hymns and their tunes are as precious to me as some of the finest poetry. This was my beginning of learning of what I call 'recital theology', of discovering that hymns can convey a depth and awareness that dogmatics often fail to do, for the hymns are dealing with the heart as well as the mind, with worship more than analysis.

Throughout my life there has been a slowly growing awareness of a greater depth and an abiding Presence in this very extraordinary world of ours. There is no sudden illumination but rather points where a little more light is revealed. There are nudges in a certain direction rather than ever taking a sure path. Nothing is forced upon me but I am offered the choice of something more than a material world. While still striving for greater awareness, I became convinced that we all belong to more than the earth. Though this earth is a wonder-filled home there is more to life than just living on this planet.

After my sister was born we moved to a house with gas light and a proper toilet. At nights we would sleep in a steel Morrison Table Shelter permanently placed in our sitting room, and eat off this metal table during the day. My only strong memory of this is splitting my head on one of the sharp corners of the shelter. In this house my brother was born. As the house was next to the railway line some of us went on the line and laid halfpennies on it. When the train went over them it 'converted' them into pennies! More often than not we lost them.

After a few years we moved again to a modern council house with electricity. We were once more near to my grandparents who had also moved. Here we would enjoy our lives as a family and in the community around us. I was aware of a lot of laughter in our house. My father in particular was quite a comedian. From this house I would go regularly up on to Alnwick Moor to enjoy the wild life and the sheer adventure of being out in the wide world.

The first time I left home, I wanted to assert my freedom, my independence. There was something I did not want to do. I was asserting my free will by being stubborn. I am sure it was something quite trivial that I was objecting to; I cannot even now remember what it was. Whatever, it made me determined to leave home. I was eight or nine at the time. My father helped me to pack a case. There were no harsh words, only what seemed a willingness to let me go. I now suspect he filled the case with anything heavy that he could find. He took me to the gate and watched me struggle down the street. By the time I got to the bottom of the street the case was too heavy for me and I was exhausted. I sat on the case and tears began to fall. I was hoping no one would notice. But my father had been watching and after a while he came to where I was and said, 'Hello, you haven't got very far. Do you want to come home?' Of course I did. He picked up the case and we returned to a welcome by my mother. I experienced the ability to walk out if I wanted to but also the loss in going. I was also made aware of the love that welcomed me back, that loved me though I had chosen to turn my back on it. Through a loving home I was learning of the love of God, though his name was rarely mentioned.

One day a friend and I went bird-nesting, not to take eggs but to enjoy the search and the wonder of the variously shaped nests, eggs and chicks. Afterwards I came home and heard a Thomas Hardy poem called 'Proud Songsters' on the radio; this gave me yet another nudge:

> The thrushes sing as the sun is going,
> The finches whistle in ones and pairs,
> And as it gets dark loud nightingales
> In bushes
> Pipe, as they can when April wears,
> As if all Time was theirs.
> 'These are brand-new birds of twelve-months' growing,
> Which a year ago, or less than twain,
> No finches were, nor nightingales,
> Nor thrushes,
> But only particles of grain,
> And earth and air and rain.'

(Thomas Hardy, *The Complete Poems*,
Papermac, Macmillan, 1976, pp. 835–6)

If you think about that you can only be filled with awe. I thrilled at finding eggs in nests, at seeing new birds and hearing bird-song, and I still do. In every egg is the mystery of life, of renewal and of creation. To hear a chick cheep within the egg was an amazing delight. How I enjoyed that wonderful world.

The world was very much a place where I felt at home and I wanted no other! Yet this visible world was interwoven with another strand I was only becoming aware of. I do not want to call it another world or even another kingdom for that implies separation and is in danger of dualism. Heaven and earth are one: God's rule of love, the kingdom of God, is here and now in the world in which we live. The world of the kingdom of God is part and parcel of this world. In reality it is better to say this world in which we live is part of God's kingdom. As people of this world we are also children of God: we live in his presence and can experience his love. The material and the spiritual are woven so finely together in a way that makes them inseparable. The visible world of matter and the invisible world of spirit are not two worlds but one. We belong to both here and now. For ease I will say we are people of two realms, of two kingdoms, but I do not want to imply separation, rather an interplay of the two that is vital to our well-being.

This is not to deny a life beyond this world, beyond what we call death. But if life is eternal we are already in it! Eternity does not come after death, though clearer vision and a fuller life may. If there is eternal life, it has begun; we have it now. What are you doing with it? We should not put off for eternity that which we are given here and now. Perhaps rather than juggle with the idea of two kingdoms you should seek to live in the eternal now. Make yourself at home in the world which God has given you and be at home with God.

As a youngster, I always wanted to know more. I liked to climb the next hill and see around the next corner. My mother said I always wanted to see the 'back of beyond'. I was never quite sure what she meant but I was often aware of a beyond or an otherness in the midst of what was obvious. While still in the junior school I asked for two special gifts on separate occasions. I wanted a telescope to look at the moon and the stars, and a microscope to look at things more closely. Pictures of snowflakes perfectly patterned, each with their own individual shape, amazed me. Because of the money spent on these – not a lot – neither the telescope nor the microscope were much of an improvement on my natural sight. The important thing was that they helped me to focus. I spent hours looking at the moon and stars in wonder. On clear winter nights I enjoyed being out, wrapped up against the cold and enraptured by what I saw. Instead of gazing at them all I concentrated on a little area at a time. It was the same with the microscope I spent ages focussing on a beetle, a leaf or a small flower, though I must admit I could never get a snowflake under the microscope without it disappearing before I could fully focus. I was learning to look long and closely at things, I was learning to focus: to give my undivided attention to something and not flit from thing to thing. Instead of it just being an object it became a subject in its own right and had something to show me or teach me. Sadly the art of giving one's undivided attention to anything, or anyone, for long is one that we are in danger of losing in a world of speed and multi-choice. We all need to practise regularly the ability of truly giving our attention to someone, or being fully focussed on what we are doing.

I was slowly learning, and I still am, that the other, and the great Other, is all around us at every moment. God does not meet us on a 'vertical' plane alone but is there on the 'horizontal' plane in which we live and move and have our being. God is not so much above us as with us. I am still growing in this awareness and relationship which is expressed in the words 'we dwell in him and he in us'.

The discovery that there is more to life than experienced by our senses can be truly a life-changing experience and free us from striving for something that is beyond our reach.

Peter Berger in his book *A Rumour of Angels* suggests that the recovery of our senses and our faith will come through the re-opening of our eyes:

A rediscovery of the supernatural will be, above all, a regaining of openness in our perception of reality. It will not only be, as theologians influenced by existentialism have greatly over empha-sised, an overcoming of tragedy. Perhaps more importantly it will be an overcoming of triviality. In openness to the signals of the transcendence the true proportions of our experience are rediscovered. This is the comic relief of redemption; it makes it possible for us to laugh and play with a new fullness.

(Peter Berger, *A Rumour of Angels*, Penguin Press, 1970, p. 119)

To keep me occupied as an active junior, I was sent to the local cinema two or three times every week. Story and adventure was something I looked forward to seeing. I saw that life was bigger than what was around me and that often it was a struggle. In the days of my growing-up nearly all films were still about good triumphing over evil and had happy endings. It would be only much later I realized that many stories were biased in favour of the conquerors, as is the writing of history. At this stage I was not aware of how often behind nice films there was a story of oppression and of land-grabbing. I now shudder to see how people are robbed of their heritage in the name of progress or by a greater power. These were the days when most films were in black and white with black-and-white thinking. Yet the cinema opened up visions of other people and different ways of living.

I was fascinated by stories of other worlds and other lives. I noticed how good usually triumphed in the end. I also saw how the greedy and the grasping caused trouble for themselves and for others. In the stories about discovering new worlds I was fascinated to discover how they were often within this world and could be come across by accident or by a searching that demanded that other things did not divert them or put them off, no matter how costly or dangerous. This was just the same as the folk tales I liked reading; many of these were sure there was another world woven into ours and just waiting to

14

be discovered. I loved the world I lived in but the feeling was still growing that there was much more to our world than this. The world is far bigger, more wonderful and more mysterious than we can even see in our dreams. Instead of 'another world' I became fascinated by this world and its otherness. The world is far deeper than any of us have fathomed. Later I would discover not only the otherness of the world but the great Other who is within it. I do not seek other worlds. I seek to know the world of the other and to share in it.

I joined the Anglican church choir. I only did so because a friend went – or so I thought. It was the week before the Fourth Sunday in Advent, the Sunday before Christmas. The choir rehearsal was at 6.30 p.m. I walked through a cold, dark churchyard full of headstones in fear and trembling. A lively imagination can often be a bother! The choir stalls were in a pool of light within a dim church, almost as far away from the door as possible. There was a feeling of moving towards the light and safety. We would spend the evening rehearsing carols but first there was an anthem to be sung for the Sunday, Purcell's 'Rejoice in the Lord always'. The words were taken from the Epistle for the coming Sunday, 'Rejoice in the Lord always and again I say rejoice' (Philippians 4.4–6). The choirmaster made us sing this 'again and again'. At one stage he came over to me while the singing was going on and said, 'Rejoice, boy! Let me see you smile when you sing this. Show that you are glad that God is here!' I found it hard to smile and look at the words, the music and to sing. But the words of the anthem became the first words of Scripture I learnt by heart. Not only were they committed to memory but into the heart. Singing over and over 'Rejoice in the Lord always', 'the Lord is at hand' and 'be anxious of nothing' in worship helped the reality to enter deeper into my being. Not only to acknowledge a Presence and rejoice in it but to smile because of it. Perhaps that is what Psalm 43 in the Book of Common Prayer means when it says: 'O put your trust in God: for I will yet give him thanks, which is the help of my countenance and my God.' Can trust in God affect not only the way you look at the world but also the way you look? Sometimes a good simple exercise is to follow the advice of my choirmaster: 'Smile, for God is here.'

That night, after the rehearsal, I could not sleep for thinking upon the words of the anthem and hearing them again and again in my mind. Years later, I would be greatly interested in 'recital theology', that is songs, hymns and rhythmical prayers that help to deepen our awareness and give us words to help us express what is in fact almost inexpressible. Prayers and hymns that have a rhythm or a beat are more easily remembered and not only help us to say something about our feelings and awareness but also deepen them. There is something about letting the words vibrate not only on our lips but also in our hearts and lives that deepens their impact. Later, only a snatch of a tune can bring back the memory of the words, the feelings and the occasion. Though some have compared this with positive thinking, I want to say it is much more than that. Some forms of positive thinking can be positively stupid! Recital theology and affirming the presence of God are to do with reality and the opening of our whole being to that reality. Positive thinking sets itself to make a series of events happen: affirmation and recital theology seek to tune to what is actual, real and happening.

Though understanding what was going on in church was still very much beyond me, the local vicar invited me to be a server on Sundays at Communion. Whether he saw some potential in me or just needed an extra helper I do not know but the devotion of this man had a lasting influence on me. He explained to me that I was to serve and that meant giving him the breads and the wine for Communion and pouring water over his hands in a washing. Easy! But he then talked to me about the sanctuary and told me I had to respect it as a special holy place. 'You should never just walk into the sanctuary without pausing and reminding yourself that you are in the presence and approaching God. Even in a church the sanctuary is a special holy place.' This was not only news – it had a wonderful air of mystery and privilege. I am still only beginning to understand this but I know having special holy places is important. If we do not have special holy places it is likely we have none. At some stage it is important to discover our own holy places.

As if to hammer this home, I was then told before I entered the sanctuary for the Communion service that there were special prayers to say. I was given these on a little printed card. It was relatively simple: there was Psalm 43 to say and a confession to make of our unworthiness, opening us up to the love and forgiveness of God. We recited alternate verses of the psalm and I loved saying, 'I will go unto the altar of God, even unto the God of my joy and gladness.' When all was done we had a short silence and only then entered the sanctuary.

This learning to pause and to wait in the presence is something I am still learning. I try to always have this pause and stillness whenever I enter a place that is called holy. Sadly today we find it hard to stop and be still. In our culture of speed and multi-choice we find it difficult to pause: we have to be forever doing something and moving on. Computers have encouraged us to expect more and more instantly, and we find it hard to wait or go slowly. Heed these words of Ruskin when he was expressing worry about people travelling fast by train:

> There was always more
> In the world
> Than man could see,
> Walked they ever so slowly . . .
> they will see it no better
> for going fast.
> (John Ruskin, *Modern Painters*, vol. 3,
> cited in Mike Graves, *The Fully Alive Preacher*,
> Westminster John Knox Press, 2006, p. 31)

At the age of 11 I went to the local grammar school. I did not do badly at school but I preferred the outdoors and found it hard to stay in to do any homework. I was prone to watch the blackbird rather than the blackboard, to listen to the song of the lark rather than my teacher. Yet I pored over a children's encyclopedia in the evenings when it was too dark or damp to go out. From early on I learnt to enjoy the gift of each new day. I would rejoice in seeing the sun rise, the first snowdrop, the buzzard flying overhead, a frog in the grass. I gave my attention to what was actually around me. I was fortunate in living so near to open countryside for there it was easy to discover the newness of each day. Later in life I would discover the wonderful prayer that is attributed to St Patrick. After affirming that we arise each day through the strength of the Trinity and in the life, death and resurrection of Christ comes the wonderful earthy affirmation:

> I arise today
> Through the strength of heaven;
> Light of sun,
> Radiance of moon,
> Splendour of fire,
> Speed of lightning,
> Swiftness of wind,
> Depth of sea,
> Stability of earth,
> Firmness of rock.

If we affirmed each day how much we depend on the earth and our environment we might learn to treat it with greater respect. When we learn to discern that God is at work in and through creation, we truly come home to the world which he has given us as our dwelling place.

Life was not all easy. At home, we never seemed to have enough money to get us through the week. The 'ticky man' came and was paid a good part of the money we owed each

Friday as soon as my dad got his pay. This left us short for the week ahead and we borrowed from the 'ticky man' once again. From the age of about 14, to help out, I got odd jobs such as working for a butcher on Saturdays and for a fish-and-chip shop owner some evenings. I would walk over half a mile to the station to collect his supply of fish and return it to the shop by sack barrow; for this I got threepence and a bag of chips! Even when I had to make two journeys the payment was the same. By the time I was 15 I realized that the home needed me to work and earn money rather than to be at school. Foolishly, I left school a few months before sitting my O-level exams; in other words I left with no qualifications. Though none of my relatives worked in the mines, I decided to get a job working at the local colliery. Life never stands still and I was entering a new stage, with new challenges and opportunities even though sometimes it might have seemed a step backwards.

Thought

> If your two parents hadn't bonded just when they did – possibly to the second, possibly to the nanosecond – you wouldn't be here. And if their parents hadn't bonded in a precisely timely manner, you wouldn't be here either. And if their parents hadn't done likewise, and their parents before them, and so on, obviously and indefinitely, you wouldn't be here.
>
> (Bill Bryson, *A Short History of Nearly Everything*,
> Black Swan, 2004, p. 480)

Exercises

Spend some time giving thanks that you exist.

Give thanks for your relationships and their love.

Trace your life, your family tree, meetings of people, into the distant past. Without just one of them you would not exist.

Alternatively, trace the tree of life. Look at evolution. In each of us the whole history of the world is reflected. What great energies have been at work to form and shape you. You are part of a great network of wonder-full influences and once you were part of 'an exploding star'! Rejoice in the mystery and wonder that is you.

Here are some words from Thomas Traherne to think upon:

> Your enjoyment of the world is never right, till every morning you awake in heaven; see yourself in your Father's Palace; and look upon the skies, the earth, and air as Celestial Joys; Having such a reverend esteem of all as if you were among the Angels.

Now there is a challenge. Do you see yourself in your 'Father's Palace'? Are you aware that you are in his kingdom? Let us journey together into a deeper knowledge that we are living in two kingdoms.

Pray

> Almighty God, you created the heavens and the earth, and made us in your own image: teach us to discern your hand in all your works and your likeness in all your children; through Jesus Christ our Lord, who with you and the Holy Spirit reign supreme over all things, now and for ever.
>
> (Collect for Second Sunday Before Lent, *Common Worship*)

> Grant us a vision, Lord, that we may see your presence with us and about us. Make us aware of you and what you want us to do. Guide us that we may be the people you have called us to be.

More to life than this

When I began to search for the meaning of life, I was first attracted to the pursuit of wealth and leisure. As most people discover there is little satisfaction in such things, and a life orientated to the gratification of greed or killing of time is unworthy of our humanity. We have been given life in order to achieve something worthwhile, to make good use of our talents, for life itself points to eternity. (Hilary of Poitiers, *On the Trinity*)

On my first day at the pit, I learnt how to clock into work and clock out at the end of a shift. I shared my lunch break drinking stewed tea and eating jam sandwiches with other young workers. There was a canteen but to take our own bait was quicker and cheaper. My first job was to work on the screens at the pit head. This was not a glamorous film shoot, but rather it was screening coal. This meant spending the whole day picking stones out of the coal that had been dropped on to a conveyor. It was the dullest of work and yet it gave me time to think about what I ought to be doing with life. I was sure there was more to life than this! No one should have to spend most of their waking hours picking up little bits of stone day after day. In fact this process has now been mechanized in many places where coal is still dug from the earth.

After a short while of working on the surface, I went for training at Ashington in Northumberland to prepare me for working underground. I was among some of the last youngsters that went down the mine at 15 years old. I was offered the opportunity to go to the technical college a day each week. Here I immediately gained good reports for my work. This made me think of becoming a mining surveyor. From the start I found working underground a wonderful and mysterious place and a place where you depended on each other for safety as well as for the production of coal. I learned how to harness the pit ponies and to use them. I gained certificates to say I could be in charge of certain mining machinery. I was also shown how to use a shovel properly as well as how a Davy Lamp worked in detecting gas. I discovered how pit props were used and how important it was to follow rules of safety. Everyone who went down the mine left a tally at the pit head when they collected their lamp and on coming back to the surface the tally would be returned to another place. At all times this meant it was known how many men were down the mine and who they were. It was a symbol of care for each person and their safety.

When my initial training was over I went to work underground at Shilbottle Colliery. Here the seams were very small and men had to work lying on their side to gain much of the coal. I became a putter, which is a like human donkey; there were no longer four-legged donkeys at Shilbottle. The putter's job was to see that pit props and other materials were put in place for the men working at the coalface. I never had to actually work on the small enclosed area where the coal hewers were. I had a reasonably good height to work in, though I liked to explore the coalface every now and again. I enjoyed the camaraderie of the mine. I learnt to arm-wrestle, had an attempt at chewing tobacco and sang my way into work with some of the other young miners. I would spend some of my spare time in their company.

When my work moved to the quite lonely job of working on my own looking after a large conveyor belt filling pit tubs, there was a telephone to keep me in contact with other people at various points along the conveyor. My friend Kemma used to ring me from work further into the mine and play me the latest tune he had learned on his harmonica. Sadly Kemma later paid the price of coal by being killed in a mining accident.

Working on my own introduced me to a great deal of silence. There were machines running and coal falling noisily into tubs but that became a sort of background noise. It left my mind undisturbed by many attractions. I learnt to concentrate on things around me and to notice them for the wonderful things they often were. I was hundreds of feet underground working in what had once been a tropical forest on the surface of the earth. Over the millennia this forest had been covered by the sea and then the sea had dried up and forests grew again. There were layers of limestone and sandstone from the sea, layers of coal from the forests, in some places there was granite from times of volcanic eruptions. Each had a story to tell and a story that lasted for thousands of years. I became aware of how wonderfully the world is made.

One night I was set to work on a new conveyor. All the work was as before but the roof above my head was made up of hundreds of thousands of molluscs that had been fossilized in one of the great changes in our earth's climate. These living creatures had rested here over millions of years and had never been seen by the human eye before this time. A special thrill went through my whole being as I contemplated the wonder of it all. The world is far fuller of mystery and wonder than any of us can dream of. Here were some early forms of life that made way for our lives upon this earth. There are so many things that are beyond explanation. I am quite happy with the idea of evolution but I am certain there is more to human life than some scientific *theory*; I purposely do not use the word explanation.

Many a morning, the sheer fact of coming out of the darkness of the mine into the bright sunlight of the world above was a thrill. It made me see the world with a radiant freshness, a radiance that is there for us all to enjoy. I wanted to share my

25

wonder of life and to explore its mysteries further. Some mornings before going home I would stop off in a spring-fresh wood, listen to the birds and admire the bluebells. I would pick a few primroses to take to my mother. I found a glory in the new day and what was about me. I did not try to make one thing better than another but enjoyed or endured what came to me. Years later, when reading about the poet Wordsworth, these words would inspire me:

> What is necessary first for visionary power is an undaunted appetite for liveliness – to be among the active elements of the world and love what they do to you, to love 'to work and to be wrought upon'; to be 'alive to all that is enjoyed and all that is endured', to have the loneliness and the courage to take in not only joy but dismay and fear and pain as modes of being without bolting for comfort or obscuring them with social chatter.
>
> (Alec King, *Wordsworth and the Artist's Vision*,
> Athlone Press, London, 1966, pp. 20–4)

In the same way, even later still, from the world of Celtic folk tales I would rejoice to hear a tale in which the Fianna-Finn are talking of music.

'What is the finest music in the world?' asked Fionn of his son, Oisin.

'The cuckoo calling from the tree that is highest in the hedge,' he answered. They went around the room, and each told what music they believed to be finest. One said the belling of a stag across the water, another the baying of a tuneful pack heard in the distance, and others believed the finest music to be the sound of a lark, the laughter of a girl, and the whisper of a loved one.

'They are good sounds all,' said Fionn.

'Tell us,' one of them asked him, 'what do you think?'

'The music of what happens,' said Fionn, 'that is the finest music in the world.'

Certainly what was happening in my life was making me think and react. I was often being overawed by all that was around me. I did not want to rush from one event to another but to enjoy things in depth. I was struggling to focus on where I was or who I was with. I wanted to give my attention fully to what was about me. Though I write this now, the feeling was far vaguer than I make it sound. I was coming up for 17, and at this stage was attracted back to the local church. I could not make much sense of the services but I was attracted by a sense of wonder. Living in a small council house, I can remember being inspired by the stillness and the size of St Michael's church in Alnwick. Once more I would serve at Holy Communion after a gap of about five years. I was able to go from working in dark, damp surroundings underground in a coal mine to assist at an altar that was flanked by four golden angels. Once again, I was only to enter the small sanctuary of this side altar after I had recited Psalm 43. I soon knew this off by heart, and I mean heart for I did not learn it by rote for my head and memory, I learnt it in worship, in awe and adoration of God. There was something quite wonderful about leaving the coal mine behind and saying:

> O send out thy light and thy truth that they may lead me:
>   and bring me unto thy holy hill and to thy dwelling.
> And that I may go unto the altar of God, even unto the
>   God of my joy and gladness.
>   (Psalm 43.3–4, Book of Common Prayer)

I learnt my unworthiness before God and confessed it before him but also through God's grace and goodness I could enter his sanctuary with joy. I was discovering how God loved me as a person and that I could have a relationship with him. The old priest at Alnwick managed to help me to understand my early strivings in the faith not so much by words but by his own actions and reverence.

My father found it strange that I should put myself out for weekday worship and at what he called 'ungodly hours', especially as I was on shift work and had to put myself out a great deal to be there. At this stage I was learning that discipleship needed discipline as well as a teacher. I was also slowly learning that if you find a holy place, the presence of God goes with you and all places are holy. There was this nudging of my life in a certain direction and yet I cannot say why this should be. Something more than the words that were said, the space between the words often spoke louder. Something, Someone, was calling . . . nothing definite (is it ever?). Due to this worship before the golden angels, the poem by Francis Thompson has always meant a great deal to me.

> Not where the wheeling systems darken,
> And our benumbed conceiving soars! –
> The drift of pinions, would we hearken,
> Beats at our own clay-shuttered doors.
> The angels keep their ancient places; –
> Turn but a stone, and start a wing!
> 'Tis ye, 'tis your estrangèd faces,
> That miss the many-splendoured thing.

Yet alongside this, life went on as it does. I was a young man earning money, with new opportunities of leisure and pleasure. I was given a freedom that I never had before because I had a pay packet, though I did hand it nearly all over to help in the upkeep of our home. I was able to go to the local dances and, from the age of 16, the local pubs. I had many a good night out with my fellow workers. We would spend most of our money at the weekends and from Monday to Thursday look for other pursuits. There was a local hall where we could meet up and go dancing for free once a week. Life was usually a healthy balance of work, rest and play, though there were some times when it went awry. I began to work regularly on night shift, from midnight until eight in the morning. In the day time I had the freedom and I would not miss out on a long walk in the sunshine. Then I went to a dance in the evening. Once I can remember going back into work after a dance and after being awake about 36 hours. I was genuinely quite tired! My task at this point was looking after a conveyor belt carrying coal and keeping the underneath of the conveyor clear. This meant shovelling a fair deal of the time and I actually fell asleep while shovelling coal. I only awoke when I fell over!

Amid this whirl of 'being alive' to all that was around me, I began to feel that there was still something missing in my life. Surely life was not meant to go on like this all the time. I needed to have some purpose, life needed a goal. There was nothing clear in this, it was not about a better job or more money, it was not even about planning for the future but it was an inner feeling that life was made for more than what I was doing. Life had depths and mysteries that I had not yet found a way of entering.

One morning when I left the mine I met my father at a local café. It was the Corner Café in Alnwick. He often went there for a cup of tea after his wagon was loaded for a journey. I know I was tired and my father was anxious to get going with his load. As I put a cup of tea in front of him I said, 'I want to be a vicar.'

My father's response was, 'You silly b......! Go and get yourself some sleep and see if you can talk some sense.'

I do not know why I had said it. I was hardly well schooled in the Church or in anything else for that matter. So I did as I was told and went home to sleep. I put it at the back of my mind but it was there, this strange idea. I could hardly say it was a call. I did not find clergy attractive or the church services stimulating but something was saying this is what I should do. I would later write with hindsight:

In the night, across the years;
You have called my name,
In my laughter and my tears.
The words are never quite the same,
Seeking out my dulled ears;
Wanting me to rise and wake,
To cast away my doubts and fears.
Your love is there for me to take;
More than this, I should know,
When the day is turned to night,
You are there, wherever I go,
My love, calling me to light.
Calling me at every breath,
Calling me to rise from death.

About the same time as saying, 'I would like to be a vicar', I went with my Aunt Connie to see *The Student Prince* in which Mario Lanza sang that he would walk with God each day. I cannot now remember much about this film but I was amazed at the idea that you could walk with God. This was one of those moments of illumination, another nudge at a great potential. Aunt Connie bought a 78 rpm recording of Mario Lanza for her gramophone so I heard the words again and again. For me the action of walking with God was actually mind-boggling and still is. To discover that God is not far off and that prayer is not a long-distance phone call seeks from us a reaction. Only later would I discover in Celtic prayers an expression of joy in walking with God:

My walk this day with God,
My walk this day with Christ,
My walk this day with Spirit,
The Threefold all-kindly:
Ho! Ho! Ho! the Threefold all-kindly.
My shielding this day from ill,
My shielding this day from harm,

30

> Ho! Ho! both my soul and my body,
> Be by Father, by Son, by Holy Spirit:
> By Father, by Son, by Holy Spirit
>
> Be the Father shielding me,
> Be the Son shielding me,
> Be the Spirit shielding me,
> As Three and as One:
> Ho! Ho! Ho! as Three and as One.
> (*Carmina Gadelica* III, p. 49)

I would also meet people who walked and talked with God in a most natural way and not just in church or in the words of the Church. God was not far off and his kingdom was at hand waiting for us to enter into it. I was slowly learning that Christianity was not a set of dogmas or about 'a happy land far, far away', but rather about a relationship with the living God here and now. Faith is not just about reciting the creed but also about walking with God and talking with God as we live our ordinary, daily lives. It is having a living, truly vital relationship with our Maker and Redeemer.

Yet at this stage nothing was clear. Is it ever? I had put the thought of 'being a vicar' to the back of my mind but it was there and surfaced now and again. In the end, at the advice of my mother, I went to see the vicar of St Michael's. Though I served at church and he knew me quite well I had never come to his door with a request. I was very nervous. He kindly asked me why I had come. 'I want to be a vicar', I blurted out in my anxiety. He saw this was something to be dealt with in the vicarage rather than on the step and invited me in. Though he knew the answer, he asked me if I was confirmed. I did not know what he was talking about. He gently explained if I was ever to become a vicar in the Church of England, I would have to get confirmed and I would have to attend classes for that purpose. I would also have to come to church a lot more often than I was. At the time I was serving once a fortnight midweek and not attending any other time. He also suggested that he taught me Latin! The only reason for this was to keep a regular contact and for him to exercise his love for Latin.

I was willing to jump through any hoops he would set me so I assented to everything, though from the start there were setbacks. I had left school at 15 and had no qualifications. I would have to get some qualifications and the technical college would only partly meet this. It was decided to get me confirmed and into the way of more study and then see how we would go from there. I was also asked to teach in Sunday school. Looking back on this, it worries me how we often get people to teach the faith who do not as yet know it. This may be a great learning curve for the teacher but it is beset by so many dangers for the pupils. My teaching was to get a lesson out of a book and repeat as best I could. I was not even advised on how to do this. Yet now and again some one would say to me later in life, 'You taught me in Sunday school.' God's grace works even in our weakness and ignorance.

After a few months and with no progress in what would happen next, I was at the vicarage when another local clergyman called. He was told of my desires and of my lack of qualifications. He suggested that the Society of the Sacred Mission at Kelham might be the place for me. Though he was not talking directly to me, my ears pricked up. He said,

> It is a bit like the commando course of the Church of England. It is quite a tough place where the men have to totally look after themselves and do a good deal of manual work. They do, however, take young men with few qualifications or no qualifications and train them up.

The 'commando course of the Church of England' was a wonderful description to my ears in the sense that it showed a Church alive and ready for action. Too often the Church appears like ancient generals talking of past campaigns when we should be more like the SAS troops trained for action and ready to battle now against the evils of our world. It not only sounded manly but a short cut in the road to what I felt called to do. I nervously said, 'I think I might like to try and go there.' After a fair bit of conversation it was decided that I should write and that my vicar should write and see if it were even a possibility.

The whole idea excited me but also filled me with anxiety. I had hardly ever left home except for holidays with friends or relatives. Yet there was something in me that said life is meant to be adventured. We are not meant to stay safe and cocoon ourselves against change or movement. Life is made up of change and movement and to refuse this is to stagnate and die. I have always been attracted by coming to the edge of a cliff, to the seashore or a new horizon as each would fill me with the wonder of what might be beyond. Frontiers are exciting places and everyone should be encouraged to enjoy them: we should learn to explore the borderlands of our lives.

Thought

There is not in the world, a kind of life more sweet and more delightful, than that of a continual walk with God; those only can comprehend it, who practise and experience it. Yet I do not advise you to do it from that motive, it is not pleasure we ought to seek in this exercise; but let us do it from the motive of love, and because God would have us so walk.

(Brother Lawrence, *The Practice of the Presence of God*,
H. R. Allenson, 1906, pp. 33–4)

Exercises

Start to practise, each day, your walking and talking with God. Get to know that God is always with you. You may like to learn 'The Journey Prayer' from the *Carmina Gadelica*:

God, bless to me this day,
God, bless to me this night;
Bless, O bless, Thou God of grace,

Each day and hour of my life;
Bless, O bless, Thou God of grace,
Each day and hour of my life.
God, bless the pathway on which I go,
God, bless the earth that is beneath my sole;
Bless, O God, and give me Thy love,
O God of gods, bless my rest and my repose;
Bless, O God, and give me Thy love,
O God of gods, bless my rest and my repose.
(*Carmina Gadelica* III, p. 179)

Remember, I pray you, what I have often recommended to you, which is, often to think on God by day, by night, in your business, and even in your diversions. He is always near you and with you: leave Him not alone. You would think it rude to leave a friend alone who had come to visit you; why then must God be neglected?

(Brother Lawrence, *The Practice of the Presence of God*,
H. R. Allenson, 1906, p. 51)

Pray

God be in my head, and in my understanding
God be in my eyes, and in my looking
God be in my mouth, and in my speaking
God be in my heart, and in my thinking
God be at my end, and at my departing.
(*Sarum Book of Hours*, 1514)

Responding to the call

—•◆•—

I don't know Who – or what – put the question, I don't know when it was put. I don't even remember answering. But at some moment I did answer *Yes* to Someone – or Something – and from that hour I was certain that existence is meaningful, and that, therefore, my life, in self-surrender, had a goal.

(Dag Hammarskjöld, *Markings*, Faber & Faber, 1964, p. 169)

There is no doubt we cannot respond to the call of God unless we are willing to face change and uncertainty. If we are to give our lives to God, we need to allow him to direct us and change us. This is what is asked of us in the word 'repentance'. To repent is to be asked to turn in a new direction, to have your sights set on different things from what they were set on before, or at least to see things in a different way. Instead of going in any direction we are now given an aim and a purpose. It means that life is meaningful and has a goal – yet, as humans, quite often, where the meaning and goal is has to be sought for over and over again. Yet from the outset the feeling of being called will alter our mindset and sense of values: the eternal has broken into our sense of time, the beyond is now known, at our highest moments, to be in our midst. Still more is required of us for if we are to serve God we must see that our will is also directed towards the works of God. We are to show our response not only in words but in our actions and in our lives. This decision to give of ourselves is not a once-and-for-all event but will need to be made throughout our lives. This change will not only change us but will change the relationship of many people to us.

Anyone who has found a purpose in life is blessed. The actual fact of life having a meaning and a goal gives us energy as well as joy. Too often people look back at 'the road not taken'. Throughout our lives opportunities are offered to us and we have to choose to take them or not. This is not a matter of one choice; we have to make many such decisions all our lives. The first choice we are given is to live: not just to exist but to be alive to the world around us and to our own being. To be alive means also to be capable of change. When Jesus met Peter he said to him, 'You are Simon son of John. You are to be called Cephas (which is translated Peter)' (John 1.42). He saw Simon not for just what he was but for the potential that was in him. Sadly many people never even come close to their potential: they fail to be the people they have the power to be. Often as life goes on that power can atrophy through lack of use or no longer be listened to because we have turned a deaf ear. Through our own lack of vision, through inattentiveness, laziness or fearfulness we fail to launch out into the deep and so we live our lives in the shallows. Sometimes by human error we have chosen the second best or an easier task but as long as we are alive there is still potential for change and to walk in newness of life.

We should not think of one vocation above another, for there are of necessity a variety of tasks to do and lives to live within them, if the world is to work in harmony. Some are called especially to be parents, others to labour with their hands, others to work in offices and yet others to act as professional carers; all are important to the well-being of the world. All of us by our birth and our upbringing have been prepared for something. Though in a world that often misses the target, other people can thwart what we were truly called to be. The climate in which we are born, the fact of poverty, and lack of a decent education can restrict us in our potential. Yet whatever the circumstances we can still fulfil some role within our society. Above all we need be attentive to what is around us and keep ourselves open to any call.

On the train from Northumberland to Kelham all sorts of doubts and fears filled my mind. From coal mine to monastic establishment was a mega-step and I was not sure I should be taking it. How had I got myself into this? Yet there was another deep feeling that said I had at least to test this out. I walked down the drive to Kelham Hall full of foreboding and quite unprepared for what lay ahead. I felt so small in this large place. God certainly chooses the foolish to help in his work of salvation. I only hoped that the potential that someone had seen was there within me.

Kelham Hall is a strange building to find in the Nottinghamshire countryside. It definitely has the feel of the Gothic. It was designed by Gilbert Scott and very much on the same lines as his design for St Pancras in London. If it had been foggy I would have let my imagination run riot with ideas of zombies and vampires! It felt rather surreal and definitely unsettling. This would be the largest house I had ever stayed in. When added to this there were about a hundred cassocked figures that were moving around in silence for much of the time, I had the feeling I was in another world to the coal mine and our little council house. I was completely out of my depth. I got lost in the size of the house and in the silences of the community.

I was even more lost in the time I shared in the round of daily worship. To go to worship at least five times every day was something I had never experienced. I was later to discover that giving God his glory was the priority, for you cannot talk about God if you do not get to know him.

God is not a theory about existence, but is ground of all being. Until we know this for ourselves in faith, in a living personal relationship with him, we will not be able to communicate it to others. We are to be people of God and not of some religion or theory about God. This relationship with God is not confined to what we do in church; it is to do with all of life. Yet if we do not have a time when we especially talk to him, and a place where we arrange 'to meet', it is likely we will let him become edged out, not only out of priorities but out of our lives. We must make sure we meet up regularly with the God who is ever present.

Christianity is not about a set of beliefs; it is about our relationship of love with our God. In this sense it is not just worship; it must also involve us in seeking to do his will. It is here on this earth God has given us life. It is in our relationship to his creation, in being sensitive and in awe of the wonders of his world, in our dealings with each other that we give glory to God. It is in the midst of life's joys and sorrows, in our failures and successes, in all the ups and downs and complexities of life that we are asked to walk in faith. We need to take to heart the words of Micah 6.8: 'What does the Lord require of you but to do justice, and to love kindness, and to walk humbly with your God?' Once again this brings me back to the idea of walking with God. Wherever life takes us, whatever happens to us our God is with us, and wants us to know him, his presence and his power. It is only when we come to know him we can give him glory and seek to serve him and proclaim his love.

This would be developed for me through *The Principles of the Society of the Sacred Mission*. The title page of *The Principles* had: 'Fear God and give glory to Him; for the hour of His judgement has come.' God is of the now, as is his judgement. We should not put off either to a future date. God asks us to live fully for him in the now. This why I like the words of Irenaeus when he says, 'The glory of God is a living man; and the life of man is a vision of God.'

The next page of *The Principles* had only the Society's motto: *Ad Gloriam Dei in eius voluntate*, 'To the glory of God in doing his will'. It is not easy for us to discern God's will but the more we seek to walk with him and talk with him, the more hope we have of discovering his will, which is bound up with love. The page that was the beginning of *The Principles* states:

> By this you were created – the Will of God. And to this end – the Praise of His Glory. You will be judged by what you are, and what avail will it be to you at the last, if you have glorified God very little in yourself, that you have talked of His Glory in many lands?

Now that is something we all need to take to heart. But all of this is jumping ahead to something I was to learn slowly and still am learning. Let me return to my first experiences of Kelham.

The chapel was built of golden-red-brown bricks. The roof was a grey concrete dome and was the second largest concrete dome in England. It looked more like a church from the Middle East than from the Nottinghamshire countryside and yet it seemed to fit its surroundings well. Inside the square building with its great central dome there was a black polished floor and little natural light. The apse had a hint of the blue of eternity. The whole effect was feeling of greatness rather than largeness, of entering space rather than being confined by it. The dimness of the interior gave the place a Byzantine feel, a feeling of mystery and awe. There was a lingering trace of the smell of incense in the air telling that 'God is here' and that here he is worshipped.

The great arch of the rood at the entrance to the sanctuary, also of brick, supported Sargeant Jagger's powerful, green, bronze, crucified Christ with his mother Mary and St John in attendance. Later I would learn that Father Stephen Bedale used to love telling the story of a 'perfect little ruffian' who looked at the Christ and said, 'Gee, ain't he tough!' This Christ was certainly no weakling. Here was a Christ who was in control. The cross, though it had been a sign of defeat, in Christ becomes the symbol

41

of victory. Here is not only the triumph over death but the victory of love over hatred, of God over all the powers that would diminish us. Here kneeling before this mighty Saviour, I would learn that even in death we cannot fall out of the hands or the love of God.

To the left of the rood arch was an equally powerful Virgin with a very strong young child supported on her left hand. They looked as if they came from strong peasant stock. Though there was mystery and awe here it was not wishy-washy; there was a sense of strength and purpose to be found in all. There was a feeling that this was not a place to dream as much as a place to dedicate yourself to the mighty work of God.

When the chapel was full of its cassocked figures and the sound of the manly singing of plainsong reverberating around the dome, the feeling of strength and purpose was increased. Was this the place where they trained men to be the 'front troops' of the Church and its outreach? It certainly felt so, with young men joyfully dedicating themselves to work and worship. But there was more; there was a feeling that here time was suspended for we were giving our attention to God in the now, and that now was in eternity.

I knew as the plainsong vibrated around me, if I was accepted, I had come to a place that would change my life forever. For me the building, the singing in plainsong by a strong body of dedicated men was totally mind-blowing. Here I would learn to die to the purposeless life and rise renewed in the service of God. It was here I would learn that it is a thin border of the imagination that separates heaven from earth, or God from us humans. Here I would discover that God is not concerned only with worship or souls but with the whole of life and with all of his creation. At every moment God keeps before us an open door. In all of life, there are always opportunities to know him, delight in him and serve him. This is not a God confined to church and worship but one who is to be met in the whole of his creation. Again later, I would rejoice to read these words by one of the Kelham Fathers:

> Christianity is not concerned with just one aspect or department of human life, but the whole of it. The Church is, or ought to be, concerned not only with how men pray, but with how men make boots, with how men fight, with how men make laws, fall in love, play football, and write sonnets.
>
> (Father Stephen Bedale SSM, speaking at the Kelham reunion, quoted in the SSM Christmas quarterly in 1922)

For me this way of looking at our faith helped to ground it and yet at the same time elevate it to a new level, opening up all of life to the eternal.

In the refectory the tableware was of stainless steel, all plates shone and if not used properly could clatter. There was no danger of breakage: in fact I believe some are still being used by the SSM in one of their houses. In many ways they were symbolic of the Society, not at first sight an economy but practical, with a willingness to risk being different. To eat in silence and to move around in silence was a new experience. I was fortunate that I was used to and enjoyed the silence of the mine. But a silence among a group of people was quite different. There was a feeling of something that spoke far stronger than words. Again this was something about the purpose and dedication of these men.

I had come for interviews with five other prospective students. I knew that my qualifications were below par. I felt I was totally out of place, as was my Northumbrian accent. A small crumb of comfort came from an elderly member of SSM who was from my home town of Alnwick and asked questions like, 'Do you enjoy playing football?'

I tried to be sincere in my interviews and talked of the strong and yet vague feeling I had of a call to the ordained ministry. Often with the questions I was asked, I was not really sure what

I was being asked and had to say so. In between interviews I walked by the River Trent, with some of the other candidates. I was aware of how much more some of these candidates knew of what they felt called to do. I saw students not only studying but playing football, and doing house chores, working in the garden and on the land. I shared a little in the washing-up after the main meal. In all I was aware of a community that worked with a joy and with a purpose. It was all over in a few days. I was promised by the prior a written reply of my acceptance or not within eight days.

I waited back in Alnwick for 12 days without much hope and yet with a degree of excited anticipation. Once day eight had passed I began to have less hope. This was in the golden age of Kelham where there were plenty of professed and new novices and there was only room for a small intake of new students from a large number of applicants. In the 1950s there was still a feeling for many that Christianity was a heroic and challenging way to follow. 'Vocation' and 'calling' were words and ideas regularly put before young people within the Church. Today it often feels as if the Church has lost its confidence: does that mean it no longer walks with faith, in living relationship with God?

While waiting I thought, 'Here is the answer to any idea of calling. If they say "No", I can forget it and get on with my life as normal. I can forget the monastery and stay in the mine and become a surveyor.' There was part of me that would have liked to hear a 'No' and put the responsibility of choosing on to someone else. Yet there was a bigger part of me saying I had to go ahead with this whatever the results from Kelham. The frightening thing is how our way forward or not is so often in other people's hands. As all decisions are made by humans there is always room for error or lack of vision.

It was another morning in the Corner Café; my father met me as I came from work. He held up the small envelope, which he had opened and read! 'Here it is. You've had it, son!' A wave of relief came over me; I thought I had been rejected. But my father explained as he gave me the letter I had been accepted. This small piece of paper would change my life forever. Strangely the relief that I had felt turned to joy, though tinged with a good deal of anxiety. I would now have to start making plans to leave behind all that was familiar and step out into the unknown.

My mother was overjoyed, as was my father though he still thought it was all a little strange. They never queried the fact that they would lose any income from me, and the fact that I might need some financial support. They wanted me to be free to do what I felt I must do. In their love for me they were willing to let me go even though it would mean a loss to them. Often when people would talk of the sacrifices I had made to go to Kelham, I could see none. I was doing what I wanted to do. It was my parents who were making the sacrifice for me. Once again a sign of their outpouring love. It was in the power of this love that I was able to reach out.

Now that I had been accepted for training I had to come out into the open. It was time to tell my workmates and friends what I planned to do. There was, as you would expect, a mixed reaction. Some thought I had gone mad, others said how wonderful it must be to have something that you really wanted to do. From now I got a lot of friendly ribbing from those I worked with. Some wondered if they should still swear in my presence or if I would still go out and have a pint with them. The answer to both of those was in the affirmative. I wanted my friends as they truly are and not as a pretence for me. Fortunately, most life went on as normal. To my surprise, the principal of the technical college at Ashington gave me a wonderful reference and showed a great deal of insight into what I was called to do. In the end it was arranged I should leave the pit only a week before setting off for Nottinghamshire. Now I felt I was going into the deep end before I had learnt to swim.

Thought

Think on these words of St Augustine of Hippo:

> God from whom to stray is to fall,
> And to whom to turn is to rise up,
> In whom to remain is to rest on a firm foundation.
> To leave you is to die,
> To return to you is to come back to life,
> To dwell in you is to live.

Exercise

The 5P exercise is one of my favourite ways of meditating. I use this as a way of creating space and waiting upon my God. It is called 5P because each part of the exercise begins with an action starting with the letter P.

Pause, Presence, Picture, Ponder, Promise

Pause   It is important to stop and let go of what you are doing. Give yourself a break from constant activity and justification by works. Let go and let God have a chance to speak. Remember God speaks most to those who can keep silent. Let the stopping be not only of words and actions, let it be a stilling of your heart, mind and body. Do a check over your body, is it relaxed? Let go of all tension out of your hands, feet, neck; be still and at ease. Let your mind relax. You may need a word or a sentence to help you do this.

Say quietly, 'Come, Lord God, I am open to you.' And repeat it with each breath.

Breathe deeply . . . . slowly . . . . comfortably.

'Come, Lord, I am open to you.'

Be still . . . .

Presence   Know that God is with you and speaks to you.

This is the reason for creating this space, not for knowledge, not even for peace, or for love, for God himself who comes to you. (No doubt you will then receive his gifts also.) God is with you, rest in his presence. Seek to be aware of the great mystery of God that is about you and within you. God will not force himself upon you, you need to open your life to him. You cannot imagine the Presence or create it for it is there but you can open your life to him.

Try and relax in the presence as you would in the sun on a nice day.

You can say quietly: 'You, Lord, are here . . . You, Lord, are with me . . . You, Lord, love me . . .

'I give myself, my love to you.'

Picture   Read Isaiah 6.1–8. Try and picture the scene. Uzziah was a good king: he ruled for 50 years, he kept peace within his kingdom. Uzziah was Isaiah's patron and protector: he was like a father to Isaiah. Uzziah became a leper. How Isaiah must have prayed for his healing but it was not to be. In the year 793 BC Uzziah died. The throne is empty, the king is dead. Isaiah enters the throne room and looks at the empty space. There is trouble ahead for the throne is empty and the king is dead. Isaiah's own position and future are in danger for the throne is empty and the king is dead. Isaiah feels as empty as the throne. The throne is empty and the king is dead. He looks at the throne and suddenly it is empty no more. 'I saw the Lord sitting on a throne, high and lofty; and the hem of his robe filled the temple.' The Lord is there. God is in control: Isaiah is not alone. Here Isaiah is aware of the holy God and in God's presence feels his unworthiness but God accepts him and blots out his past sin. Now God calls: 'Whom shall I send, and who will go for us?' Not an order but a question. Isaiah's life will never be the same again. He replies, 'Here am I; send me!'

Ponder   Think how you would have reacted to such a call. Do you in fact hear God's call today? Sometimes the call is not clear; it is only expressed in a discontent with the present, with the awareness that life and our surroundings, if not the world, could be better than they are. There is always an immediacy about the call; once heard it should not be put off. We are asked to respond like Isaiah and say, 'Here am I, Lord; send me.' There is a need to know that the call comes from beyond us; it is God's call and God's will, not just a whim or a desire of our own. Seek to discover what Jesus meant when he said, 'You did not choose me but I chose you' (John 15.16). This can be the wonderful beginning of an exciting adventure.

Promise   Those whom God calls he sends. The call to move out and adventure is of its nature exciting. Too often after the call nothing happens. Promise to keep at least a little of each day open to God and say each day, 'Here I am, Lord, send me.'

Pray

> Lord God, I am no longer my own, but yours.
> Put me to what you will,
> rank me with whom you will.
> Put me to doing, put me to enduring;
> let me be employed for you,
> or laid aside for you,
> exalted for you,
> or brought low for you;
> let me be full, let me be empty;
> let me have all things,
> let me have nothing.
> I freely and wholeheartedly yield all things
> to your pleasure and disposal.
> And now, glorious and blessed God,
> Father, Son and Holy Spirit,
> you are mine and I am yours.
> So be it.

(John Wesley, 1703–91)

Living the faith

The Rood at Kelham

> This is a place for human sacrifice
> and on that altar stone young men must die.
> The green king on the great red mountain
> Cries his burden:
> Crucify
> yourselves for I am crucified. Come
> to the edge of world without ending,
> beyond the glimmer on tiles, the shadow on stone
> step over into nothing, and no returning
> except in the procession
> in and out of the arches, in festival gladness
> rejoicing in dedication and resurrection.
>
> (Brother George Every SSM,
> used with permission of SSM)

This time my arrival in October was quite different from before. I was coming to stay, to be part of a group of students, to share in a monastic way of life. I can remember the day I was to leave home and all its security. I would leave behind my job and its income, my friends and their support and companianship. I would give up the freedom to roam where I liked, to come and go as I pleased. Instead of nights out with my mates I would spent nights in prayer and silence. Instead of gaining possessions I would learn to call nothing my own. I was fearful, I was anxious, I was far from certain but I was also setting out on a great adventure. There was a strange feeling that this is what I was being called to do. Instead of having much free time I would be compelled to go to church many times each day,

I would not be allowed to speak except in worship for more than 12 hours out of every 24. It all sounded very restrictive, it would appear my life was going to be much narrower than before. For a while I felt this was so and wondered why I endured it. Why had I given up my freedom? Whenever a bell rang I had to stop doing what I was doing and answer the call to prayer. How could someone narrow their life like this? I wondered if I was becoming like a Pavlovian dog in the way I responded to certain stimuli. Only slowly, it seemed very slowly, there was a change, not in my surroundings but in me. I was beginning to discover new depths in the things I was doing and new depths in myself. I was no longer an observer looking in from the outside but a partaker in all that happened within the community.

The silence gave me time to focus on my vocation and on the wonder of the world in which I lived. There was no hiding behind loud music or a few pints. I was learning to live to the glory of God – I am still learning – and gaining glimpses of glory. Ordinary tasks were being transformed in the way that only love can transform them. I began to understand how Jacob could work for seven years for love and it would seem like a day. I was discovering how to step out of time and into eternity. I was learning that in love nothing that you give up for the beloved is a sacrifice and all that you give away enriches you. But again this is jumping ahead.

I was soon made aware that most things ran to a strict time-table. The day was laid out like this:

6.30 a.m.	Compulsory cold shower
	Morning Prayer
	Holy Communion
8.00 a.m.	Breakfast
	Room tidy
9.00 a.m.	Meditation in chapel

10.00 a.m.	Lectures and study
12 noon	Sext: the midday act of worship
	Lunch
2.00 p.m.	Afternoon work, football, time off
4.00 p.m.	Tea
	Study lectures
6.00 p.m.	Evensong
	Study
9.30 p.m.	Compline: the final service of the day

A shower before the start of day is a great idea but a compulsory cold shower is a bit strange. Did they really think it would subdue the flesh? Surely they did not think the flesh or passions were evil. Would they advocate rolling naked in the snow in depth of winter or in a bed of nettles in the summer? Some saints have done these things. I hope it was devised more to invigorate the body and to awaken us to the new day.

Meditation was new to me. I found that if I tried to empty my mind, it was like emptying a pond. There might be nice fresh water for a while. But very soon you were turning over the sludge and the deep mud. Here I was in a holy place, among dedicated people and thinking the worst thoughts of the day. The mind was not made to be empty. The only reason to try and empty the mind is to fill it with something else. There is a sense in which the mind is like a CD or DVD that cannot easily be erased. Everything you have ever done, seen, heard, read, experienced for good or for ill is recorded; all the life-enhancing and all the destructive and impoverishing experiences are there and, if you press the right or wrong buttons, they will come to the fore. Much of the time we can be in reasonable control and select what we choose. But in times of quiet, tiredness or distress the random button is often hit and all sorts of events from the past reverberate in our lives. This is often why we choose to hide behind hyperactivity and constant sound. Be still, and often the worst thoughts of the week surface. This is nothing new for here are some words from a monk of the tenth century:

Shame on my thoughts,
How they stray:
They'll bring me trouble
On Judgement Day.

During the Psalms they are off
On a path not right
Running, misbehaving, distracted
All in God's sight.

Seeking out wild parties
With loose women in mind – sinned
Through woods and cities
Swifter than the wind.

A moment with great beauty
And loveliness on high
The next with shameful acts
I tell you truly, it is no lie.

With no boat or transport
They can cross every sea,
Around earth and heaven
Then return back to me.

They race without wisdom
Forever they do roam,
After such foolishness
They are suddenly home.

If you seek to bind them
Or shackle their feet,
They refuse to be held
Or cease to be fleet.

Sword will no tame them
Neither the strong whip.

Like an eel they slither
And slide from my grip.

No lock, prison nor chain
Will them a moment detain.
No sea, nor strong fortress
Their journeying refrain.

O Beloved, chaste Christ,
To whom all eyes are clear
May your seven-fold Spirit
Check them, keep them here.

God of the elements
Come rule my will
That you may be my love
And I do your will.

That I may reach Christ
And his holy company
They are not fickle, unsteady
Not as you see me.

But we need not despair, we just need to be more careful what experiences we record: this involves what we do, what we watch and what we seek after. Meditation is not something for 20 minutes a day, it is a way of life. Life will always have a mixture of good and evil, of joy and sorrow, of growth and of disintegration, but we can influence it all by the attitude we take and the awareness we bring to each event. Even more so when we begin to learn that God is with us wherever we are. I am always amazed that people can say in services, 'The Lord is here' or 'The Lord be with you' and not be thrilled to the core by such words. I sometimes think it would be good to say those words and leave it at that. What more do we want? This brings me back again to that Scripture passage I learnt through singing it in the choir as a small boy and the words that follow:

Rejoice in the Lord always; again I will say, Rejoice. Let your gentleness be known to everyone. The Lord is near. Do not worry about anything, but in everything by prayer and supplication with thanksgiving let your requests be made known to God. And the peace of God, which surpasses all understanding, will guard your hearts and your minds in Christ Jesus.

Finally, beloved, whatever is true, whatever is honourable, whatever is just, whatever is pure, whatever is pleasing, whatever is commendable, if there is any excellence and if there is anything worthy of praise, think about these things . . . and the God of peace will be with you.   (Philippians 4.4–9)

If the mind does go on to random selection, the more noble, right and good things we have 'recorded' there the better. The mind is very like a garden. It is no use just pulling out the weeds for if it is left empty they will return. In the end we have to fill the garden with what we want and this is the best way to suppress the weeds and prevent them from taking over. This deliberate choice is the beginning of meditation: what we focus on makes us who we are. Through meditation, I slowly learnt, we can do our daily work rejoicing in the presence and glory of God. One of the books that I used in meditation was *The Spiritual Maxims of Brother Lawrence*. Here are some of his words:

We can do little things for God; I turn the cake that is frying on the pan for love of Him, and that done if there is nothing else to call me. I prostrate myself in worship before Him, Who has given me grace to work; afterwards I rise happier than a king. It is enough for me to pick up a straw from the ground for the love of God.

(H. R. Allenson, *The Spiritual Maxims of Brother Lawrence*, London, 1906)

Not only was I learning to converse with God, I was learning that every act can be done to his glory. At Kelham, I could move from working on the cabbage patch to being at a lecture on the mystical presence of God. I could come in from playing football to write an essay on St Paul, or from scrubbing a floor to exploring the meaning of the incarnation. I could come from shovelling coal to singing plainsong to the praise of God. No act was holier than another, all had the potential of being holy, all were able to be done for the love of God.

SSM's motto was *Ad Gloriam Dei in eius voluntate*, 'Give glory to God in doing his will'. I was soon to discover that I was not only expected to pray, and study theology to the glory of God. I was expected to shovel coal, to scrub out urinals, to play football all to his glory. One wise old monk said to me, 'Remember if you are to clean urinals to the glory of God it means making sure you clean the bits that no one can see.' This was not a religion that would confine me to a building; it opened out all of life and the whole world. I could rejoice in God's creation and give glory to him. I could give him praise through my muscles and my physical actions. I could praise him on a mountain top or in a coal hole. It was not only in the study of the Bible we would find him. We could find him in the study of science or in the study of birds. If we looked close enough and deep enough all things would reveal wonder and awe and lead us to worship. This is the God we would encounter in our meetings with each other: the God to be found in friend and stranger. This was the religion of an expanding world and an expanding life. This was not a God we could enclose in a building and keep there. Here is the God of the whole of creation and all that we do. So, when religion is used to restrict life and adventure we need to look upon it with some suspicion. This is a faith that sees all work as meaningful and none need be degrading. The poet Gerard Manley Hopkins wrote:

Turn then, brethren, now and give God glory. You do say grace at meals and thank and praise God for your daily bread, so far so good, but thank and praise him now for everything. When a man is in God's grace and free from mortal sin, then everything that he does, so long as there is no sin in it, gives God glory and

what does not give him glory has some, however little, sin in it.
It is not only prayer that gives God glory but work. Smiting on
an anvil, sawing a beam, whitewashing a wall, driving horses,
sweeping, scouring, everything gives God some glory if being in
his grace you do it as your duty. To go to communion worthily
gives God great glory, but to take food in thankfulness and
temperance gives him glory too. To lift up the hands in
prayer gives God glory, but a man with a dungfork in his hand,
a woman with a slop pail, give him glory too. He is so great that
all things give him glory if you mean they should. So then, my
brethren, live.

(Taken from an address based on the opening of
'The Spiritual Exercises of Ignatius Loyola'
quoted in Gerard Manley Hopkins, *Poems and Prose*,
ed. W. H. Gardner, Penguin, 1963)

God was not remote but close to each of us. We knew our God to
be a transcendent God, yet a God that is close to us. Transcendence
declared that we could never capture God fully in words, on a
page, or in our minds; God could not be fully contained in any
thing. Yet we could discover his presence in and through all of
his creation. We could walk and talk with our God. The mind
may never fully grasp him but we can hold him in our hearts.

The influence of such ideas and words of poems, like Elizabeth
Barrett Browning's 'Aurora Leigh':

> Earth's crammed with heaven
> And every common bush afire with God,
> But only he who sees, takes off his shoes

helped me to discover that vision is about seeing! I wonder
what I had thought it was about. Prophets were known as seers
and this was as much about the insight they had as any fore-
sight. At some early stage at Kelham I decided to look closer
at all that was around me to enjoy the world. I was not here to
renounce the world but to learn to love it for I believed God
made it out of his love. I often would start the day with words

58

from Psalm 118.24: 'This is the day that the LORD has made, let us rejoice and be glad in it.'

It is a good exercise to take some part of God's creation each day and to rejoice in its mystery and wonder. With William Blake it is good to seek

> To see a world in a grain of sand,
> And heaven in a wild flower,
> Hold infinity in the palm of your hand,
> And eternity in an hour.

In time I decided to look at a different part of creation every day, to explore its depths and mystery. I would rejoice that it is not only created out of the love of God but that he uses the earth and earthly things to reveal himself to us. In the right hands, a little bit of soil can still open the eyes of the blind.

Thought

With regard to the world around one, there should be a conscious willed period of attentiveness each day. It is the will that has to be used to raise the consciousness from the depths of self to the world outside. It is important to notice positively the objects of one's environment, the things in the familiar street, the flowers and trees in the garden and park, and above all the people one passes to and fro from one's work. Each is complete in itself, but it needs our recognition, just as we need the recognition of others to be fully human. If we do not trouble to recognise others because of an inner preoccupation, no one will trouble to recognise us. It is important not only to recognise and acknowledge the uniqueness of each object and person but also to flow out to them in gratitude for being what they are. All life in awareness is a blessing, and we show this by blessing those around us. This does not require a formula or an articulated statement; it is essentially an inner gratitude.

(Martin Israel, *An Approach to Spirituality*,
The Mysticism Committee of the Churches Fellowship
for Psychical Research and Spiritual Studies, 1971, p. 28)

Exercise

Choose a different part of creation to explore and give thanks for each day. Once or twice a week take a created thing and seek to look at it in depth. Allow it to be a subject in its own right and speak for itself. Focus all your attention upon it to discover its mystery and to know that it is part of God's wonder-full world. If you varied the day each week you might like to follow this order which I took mainly from Genesis 1.

Monday: Explore the beginnings, order out of chaos, light out of darkness, the evolution of the world.

Tuesday: Give thanks for and explore the air which makes life possible, for the atmosphere in which we live.

Wednesday: Glory in the riches of water, the seas and rivers, at the miracle of the water cycle and of rain that refreshes the earth.

Thursday: Explore the mysteries of the galaxies, the glory of sun, moon and stars, the balances of day and night, tides and seasons.

Friday: Give thanks to God for life, for all living things. Seek to enjoy and discover the variety and individuality of each creature. Praise God for the diversity of life.

Saturday: Enjoy your own humanity. Explore wonders and richness of human life and relationships. Seek to treat others with awe and respect.

Sunday: Learn to relax in the presence of God. Make sure you have time off from activity. You may also like to remember this is the day of the resurrection, giving thanks for all of life and rejoicing that in God life is eternal.

Pray

Lord, increase
my zest for living,
my vision of glory,
my hearing of your call,
my grasp on reality,
my response to your love,
my sensitivity to others,
my gentleness to creation,
my taste for wonder
my love for you.

Call nothing your own

The fullness of sacrifice demands the sacrifice of all earthly goods. No brother may therefore claim anything as his own, either for possession or enjoyment; since one may not give up personal possessions and yet claim the comforts and pleasures of their use. While simple pleasures and enjoyment are not forbidden, the life of all must be kept in real simplicity and poverty, and no one should have anything that he cannot willingly lay aside.

(From 'The Constitution' of the Society of the Sacred Mission)

My new home was not over-furnished. I would share a room with two other students. Each of us would be from various years in our training. In the room were three tables and chairs and three beds. The beds had cupboards under them to contain all our clothing. The mattress was hard, the blankets were ex-army. I would only have this room for part of a year and then would have to move. The moving was easy for there were not many possessions to move. In the move we were all given new people to share our room with, the choice was not ours. We were not allowed to add any furnishings or even photographs of our own to any of the rooms. Radios were banned as such would have invaded the silence that was so much a part of the community. I was beginning to discover why some described Kelham as a 'commando course', but there would be no army-style pin-ups. Actually, as I had only brought a single case of clothing the lack of cupboard space was not a bother.

I slowly learnt the glorious freedom of calling nothing my own, that 'no one should have anything that he cannot willingly lay aside'. A wonderful lesson, for a life is so enriched when it is not measured by what one owns. It also means one can travel lightly and not be hampered by things. There is also a movement away from trust in possessions and material power to putting one's faith in God and in his might. In the end no possessions can save a person, and one day we will all be called to leave all behind. The more possessions we have the harder it is to leave them. There was a sense that everyone at Kelham learnt to travel lightly. We were discouraged from becoming too attached to things. Though I must add that this was not a turning our back on the world; rather it was a desire to enter deeper into what was around us and to look at all in the light of eternity and not just the passing moment. By not chasing one thing after another we learnt to appreciate what was about us. In not treating things as objects to possess there was a better chance of seeing them as subjects in their own right, in appreciating them for what they are. It also helped us to be ourselves rather than to measure ourselves by things around us.

I still have this image from films I have watched of people going in search of a hidden land. In discovering its treasures and wanting them some mechanism is set off that is in danger of destroying all. Then you see people trying to escape from the troubles around them. The greedy people are weighed down with gold and jewels and cannot move quickly, or they sink into swamps because of the weight they are carrying. The possessions they could let go of become the death of them. Those who travelled lightly and did not seek to possess were the ones who gained their freedom. They were only stories but so full of truths.

In a world where so many people are unfulfilled, there is a constant desire to possess more and more. This need to have so many possessions is often a reflection of our inner poverty and emptiness. If you believe that we are made by the love of God and for his love then nothing will fill the space in your heart which is for God alone. In many ways our heart reveals our eternal longings and it cannot be satisfied with things. On an earthly level you can see the same process in certain children who are given things by rich parents but are not given enough loving attention. No amount of goods will compensate for a lack of love. Many a child experiences the truth expressed by St Paul, 'without love I am nothing' (see 1 Corinthians 13.1–3).

Even more telling are the words of Jesus, 'One's life does not consist in the abundance of possessions' (Luke 12.15). The danger with measuring by possessions is that it places the emphasis on 'me' and 'mine', giving the impression that all gravitates around me. In looking at possessions, we are not so much concerned by what one has – possessions are neither good not evil – but that they become the centre of life and the centre of the universe. Expressing our lives by possessions can make us very self-centred. A Roman parable tells us: 'Whoever craves wealth is like a person who drinks sea water to quench his thirst. The more he drinks the more he increases his thirst and he ceases not to drink until he perishes.' In the Gospel of St Matthew there is a picture of a man turning his back on Jesus, who is the light of the world: we are told, 'he went away grieving, for he had many possessions' (Matthew 19.22). Sadly many a person has become possessed by their possessions and can only measure their life by what they have. What is important is not what we have but who we are. This is expressed well in an old Shaker hymn from the Appalachian Mountains.

> It's a gift to be simple,
> It's a gift to be free,
> It's a gift to come down where we ought to be,
> And when we see ourselves in a way that is right,
> We live in a valley of love and delight.

In our world it is not easy to see oneself in 'a way that is right'. A good exercise is to try and describe yourself without giving your name, your job or talking about possessions.

The joyful side to non-possessing was expressed by the early Christians who gladly shared their goods. They were described 'as having nothing, and yet possessing everything' (2 Corinthians 6.10). Being freed from the need to possess we can set our sights on what truly matters to us, not just in time but in the light of eternity. Not possessing is not just about detaching and letting go – in many ways there are too many detached people in our world – it is about positive choosing and attaching our lives to what really matters. If anyone thinks such giving up of things is a hardship they should listen to the words of St Philip of Nola:

> Think you the bargain's hard to have exchanged
> The transient for the eternal, to have sold
> Earth to buy heaven?
> (Quoted in Helen Waddell, *The Desert Fathers*,
> Constable, 1936, p. 30)

Some of this was so easy to say for in many ways we were protected in our community life. I had no rent to pay, and no bills coming in. I had more meals and more food than I would have had at home. I was not involved in having to provide money to support the way of life I was living. Study notes and writing material were provided for free and there was quite a good library with many of the books we needed. There was even a supply of some of our clothing, including a cassock and a scapular to cover it and protect it from getting too soiled. After the first term we wore a cassock all the time except when doing work for which it was not practical or sensible. Not worrying about material things gave us liberty to be, a privilege that many people did not and do not have. I hardly needed any money. In fact I managed on about ten shillings a week (50p) that was sent from home one week and from an aunt and uncle another. Out of this money I managed to save almost half of it to give away.

Everyone did some form of manual work in the afternoons. There was a small farm area producing vegetables, and pigsties with their contingent of pigs. People were needed to maintain the grounds as well as the house, to decorate as well as scrub. The chapel floor got a daily buffing if not a polish. Then there were meals to prepare, cooking to do, tables to set and all the washing-up afterwards.

Added to this all students played football in season, and tennis or cricket in the summer. I enjoyed playing football as I had played for a team in Alnwick for a short time. One of the funny football events was when our first team played against the local Borstal. The visiting lads had obviously been told to go gently with these 'delicate monks'. They came thinking the game would be a walkover. It only took about ten minutes into the game for them to realize we would give no quarter and they were up against some tough characters. As it was, we lived under tougher conditions than they did and with fewer privileges. This was always a game that both sides had to win to keep their dignity!

In true army style, I was soon given a job that suited my background. I was put in charge of the boilers. As they were coke and coal boilers, it meant I was back shovelling coal. I would have to see to the boilers at least three times a day. The first time was before I had my cold shower at 6.30 a.m. I would see to them at lunch time and again after the service of Compline at 9.30 p.m. Sometimes my afternoon job would be to see the delivery of coal or coke and then to shovel it into its right place. Perhaps I had been put on 'jankers'! However I was given a privilege for this work: I was allowed to make myself a cuppa at the end of the day. I had this as the house entered into silence.

The Silence was divided into two parts: the Greater and the Lesser Silence. The Greater Silence was when no one spoke except in worship. This silence was with us each 12 hours from

Compline at 9.30 p.m. until 9.30 a.m. after our time of meditation. As most of this time was spent in sleep or in worship there
was no difficulty. Though there were times, like Holy Week,
when the Greater Silence went on for a few days. Anyhow I was
used to working in silence in the coal mine when I worked
alone. The Lesser Silence lasted from 9.30 a.m. until after our
midday service of Sext. In this silence we were supposed to talk
only when need arose about our work or within our lectures.
The House Rule stated:

> The conversation of the brethren is meant to cheer us, but God's
> voice speaks most often in silence. Keep some part of every day
> free from all noise and the voices of men, for human distraction
> and the craving for it hinder Divine Peace.

The very last sentence was the real challenge for it said: 'He
who cannot keep silence is not content with God.' To assist in
this silence and to avoid other distractions no one was allowed
to have a radio or phone and there was no television. There
were daily papers and periodicals in the common room.

Through silence I found stillness and calm being part of each
day. But I wanted to add to this that God also speaks through
encounters with each other. God speaks to us through all sorts
of events and occasions. Often poets have spoken to me more
clearly than theologians, and scientists have filled me with awe
about creation more than those Christians who seem to suggest
the world should not be enjoyed. I still cannot understand
the Christians who would suggest that God's creation should
not be enjoyed. Christianity that is not life-enhancing, and
life-extending is not worthy of the name.

In time, another job I did regularly was to work with Brother
James. He was in charge of the printing press but also did quite
a few electrical repairs. I helped on the electrical side of the
work. Occasionally it meant being under the floor of the great
house, or scaling ladders to get on the outside of the chapel

dome as there was a system of lowering the high lamps from there. One of the privileges of this was I had my own little work-shop which contained various electrical parts. Most of this work was simply replacing light bulbs and repairing faulty lamps and switches.

The beginning of the first year of study was a struggle. I had never got into a system of regular study. I was easily distracted to follow my own path and go off reading other things. I was more at home labouring in the fields or shovelling coke and coal. I was putting my brain to so many new experiences my mind was in a whirl. At the end of the first term Father Theodore, the prior, asked to see me and warned me if I did not improve in my studies I might have to leave. I do not know if this was meant as shock therapy but it certainly worked that way. I gave far more attention to my lectures and the essays I had to write. In fact it made me focus on all around me, my worship in chapel, and my manual work around the house and grounds. I did not want to have to leave these things. In such a short time this way of life had become precious to me. Somehow I suddenly got into gear.

Kelham's aim, remember, was not just study – in fact not primarily study – but about the glory and worship of God. It all came home to me when I was asked to write an essay on 'glory'. I understood it had its roots in the Hebrew word *Shekinah*, which describes God's hidden glory (as described when Moses sought to see the face of God in Exodus 33.14–23). Interesting to think that Moses could only look on God after he passed by; glory is often discovered in retrospect when we realize God was with us, even though we were unaware at the time. The idea of glory was developed again with the Greeks and their idea of *doxa*. But as I looked at some of the great writings I was more confused for glory is beyond words. I sought to simplify it all and turned to the *Theological Word Book*. I looked up the word 'glory' and it simply said: 'see "God"'.

Perhaps this meant me to turn to another page but I closed the book up. This was a big nudge from a set of directions. To know what glory is it is necessary to see God, to know his presence in the world and to enjoy getting to know him. Hymns like 'To God be the glory', and 'From glory to glory advancing, we praise thee, O Lord', for me began to have a far deep meaning: a meaning far beyond the words.

It is a surprise to many that we were not asked to preach or even take any of the services while we were in training. We were not to be let loose until we were steeped in worship and in the presence of God. We were to preach by example more than by words; only those who live a certain way of life can truly communicate it to others. Too often today people are given the equipment of book knowledge while they have not had the experience for the words to change into the Word of Life. The very essence of Kelham's approach in this comes from *The Principles*: 'You will be judged by what you are, and what avail will it be to you at the last, if you have glorified God very little in yourself, that you have talked of His Glory in many lands?'

We were to absorb the word of God, to live it and to meditate upon it. Only after doing this for a long time could we begin to communicate it to others.

After about three and a half years at Kelham I came upon a crisis time. Suddenly words seem to lose their meaning; there appeared to be too many words and lots of analysis. I got tired of trying to say what St Paul meant by a single word. I did not want to tie him down for so often he meant not only one thing but more. I could not opt for any system that could neatly divide good and evil, or make our lives depend upon good works alone. Nor could I renounce a world which God had created or truly deny myself until I knew I had a self to deny. I was in a whirl and felt like leaving Kelham. Added to this my mother was quite poorly and often had to stay in her bed. I felt she could do with my help. But I also knew that it would hurt her terribly if I came home. So I continued to attend lectures and do essays. But in the main I opted out of theological study in the narrow sense. I avidly read William Wordsworth, the Brontës, T. S. Eliot, and D. H. Lawrence including his poetry. In these and other novelists and poets I was rediscovering a depth of feeling that I was looking for. I was learning again to 'speak what we feel and not what we ought to say'. I was also discovering from the poets how 'we feel we are greater than we know'.

One of D. H. Lawrence's sentences from *The Rainbow* spoke strongly to me. He first described the work of the farming Brangwen men who would lift their heads from the soil to the church tower, which was two miles away on a hill. As they turned again to the horizontal land, they were aware of something standing above them and beyond them in the distance.

> There was a look in the eyes of the Brangwens as if they were expecting something unknown, about which they were eager. They had an air of readiness of what would come to them, a kind of surety, and expectancy, of an inheritor.

Then in describing the women and their longings Lawrence went on to say: 'So long as the *wonder of the beyond* was before them, they could get along whatever their lot' (D. H. Lawrence, *The Rainbow*, Wordsworth Classics, 1995, p. 3, my italics). I felt I had once more to get a grip of this; I had to get behind the words and enter into the wonder of the beyond that was there in our midst, to come alive to what was around me with a degree of expectancy, knowing that I am an inheritor of the kingdom of heaven. An inheritor is not one who waits for his inheritance but one who has received it and can enjoy its benefits. I had for a little while lost contact with the wonder of the beyond. I had not been aware that in him we live and move and have our being. One of the reasons for spires and towers is to point us to the vertical, to the beyond in our midst. Every church stands solidly on the earth and yet points us to the heavens. They are to remind us there is no separation, heaven and earth are one and it is our lack of vision that makes us fail to enjoy our inheritance to the fullest. I went back to my studies with a new joy and a deeper insight into what the words were trying to do. Words are only pointers to make us look beyond them and beyond ourselves.

Final exams came and went. After them I had to go home to see my mother who was still quite ill. By now she was saying Morning and Evening Prayer every day. Though she had rarely gone to church she was also aware of the wonder of the beyond. She also saw this as a sharing in the communion of prayer with me, and with the whole Church. It was a sacrament of love not only with God but also with me. She would continue to say her daily prayers from the Book of Common Prayer until her death. Then my sister, again not a churchgoer, would 'inherit' her prayer book and say her daily prayers from it.

My exam results were not startling in any way, but I had passed and could look forward to being ordained. As I was to serve my first curacy in County Durham I would be ordained in Durham Cathedral, fortunately not too far for my parents to travel. No longer would I be free from financial worries; now I would have to pay my own bills and work for an income to provide for life as most people have to. No longer would I be protected by the rules, the walls and the strength of SSM. I was sorry to leave Kelham but also very ready to move on and into a new way of living.

Thought

Whoever is devoid of the capacity of wonder, whoever remains unmoved, whoever cannot contemplate or know the deep shudder

72

of the soul in enchantment, might just as well be dead for he has already closed his eyes upon life.

(Albert Einstein, quoted in Michael Mayne,
This Sunrise of Wonder, Fount, 1995, p. 109)

Exercise for throughout the day

On waking

Be still in the presence of God. Affirm that God is with you now.

Pray: 'As we rejoice in the gift of this new day, so may the light of your presence, O God, set our hearts on fire with love for you: now and forever.'

Throughout the day

God, you are here: open my eyes to your presence. Open my heart to your love.

In the evening

Think over the events of the day – and of your own feelings and reactions.

What gave you joy, or made you sad, or fearful? God is with you and ready to help, guide and share. Explore why you reacted in such a way and if you had forgotten or ignored what God offered to you.

The end of the day

Commend your life to God and his keeping.

Say: 'I will lay me down in peace and take my rest for it is you, Lord, that makes me dwell in safety.'

Know that God in his love is with you now, tomorrow and beyond.

Pray

Disturb us, Lord, when we are too well pleased with ourselves, when our dreams have come true because we have dreamed too little, when we have arrived safely because we sailed too close to the shore.

Disturb us, Lord, when, with the abundance of things we possess, we have lost our thirst for the waters of life; having fallen in love with life, we have ceased to dream of eternity; and in our efforts to build a new earth, we have allowed our vision of the new heaven to dim.

Disturb us, Lord, to dare more boldly to venture on wider seas where storms will show your mastery; where losing sight of land we shall find the stars. We ask you to push back the horizons of our hopes; and push into the future in strength, courage, hope and love.　　　　　　　　　(Attributed to Sir Francis Drake)

Out of the shell

The only question to ask today, about a man or a woman,
is: Has she chipped the shell of her own ego?
Has he chipped the shell of his own ego?
They are all perambulating eggs
going: 'Squeak! Squeak! I am all things to myself,
yet I can't be alone. I want somebody to keep me warm.'

(D. H. Lawrence, 'The Egotist' in
The Complete Poems of D. H. Lawrence, p. 497)

On Advent Sunday, 1959, I stood in one of the most wonderful buildings in the world. Durham Cathedral has been described as 'one of the greatest architectural experiences in Europe'. It is now also a World Heritage site. It is the only English cathedral to retain almost all of its Norman (Romanesque) craftsmanship. Standing proud on a hill above the River Wear on almost an island it points us to the great beyond in our midst.

Soon I would process down to the high altar past the magnificent mighty pillars and their decorations. I remembered that this cathedral was built not only to the glory of God but also as a shrine for the great Northumbrian, St Cuthbert. Earlier, I had gone down to Cuthbert's tomb and looked at the plain slab with 'Cuthbertus' inscribed upon it. Here were not only the bones of Cuthbert but also some remains of King Oswald, and a few bones belonging to St Aidan.

Now in cassock, surplice and white stole I stood in the Galilee Chapel at the west end waiting by the tomb of the Venerable Bede. With my fingers I traced over the letters: *HAC SUNT IN FOSSA BEDAE VENERABILIS OSSA*. Translated from the Latin, this means 'In this tomb are the bones of the Venerable Bede'. On that Advent Sunday some of the words of this great writer and historian came to mind:

> Christ is the Morning Star,
> who when the night of this world is past,
> brings to his saints the promise of the light
> of life and opens everlasting day.

The great building is the resting place of so many of the great names and saints of Northumbria. Here I was to be ordained deacon by Bishop Maurice Harland. I thanked God for all that had been at work in this place and for my coming to this point in my life, and prayed for what lay ahead. Then we were told to move off in procession. This was a great moment for my parents. Sadly my mother would not live to see me ordained priest.

As was the custom, I was sent to my first curacy by SSM; I did not choose it. I was to go to St Helen's, Auckland. St Helen was the mother of Constantine who was declared an emperor while in York. St Helen was also in York and there is a tradition that she was of British descent, though this is not likely. Yet the thought of Helen and Constantine in York set me to think of the early Christians that we know of in the British Isles: Alban, Ninian, Patrick, David, Kentigern, Serf, Columba, Baldred, Aidan, Oswald, Cuthbert, Chad and Cedd, to mention a few. To go to a church that was dedicated to a saint with links to this country, and who is credited with finding the cross of Christ, made me want to explore more of the beginnings of Christianity in this land.

The Vart family offered me a space in their home at Holme Mill, West Auckland. I would pay for my digs but what was given to me in return was beyond price. They were not church-goers, but again and again they revealed their love in their dealings with others. So often at their table were one or two people who needed to know that they were loved and that someone cared for them and their well-being. Here, like I was, they were accepted as part of the family. With them I was experiencing once more that community, love and care are not confined to Christians or a monastic way of life.

John Vart would put himself out to get me to a church three to five miles away and never expected or sought any reward. He would be there after a service to bring me back to my new home. John was a fund of information about local places. In my visit to one church he told me I was going to Jam Jar City which was part of Treacle Tin Valley. It sounded a wonderful venture. He then told me it was because the old steel workers and miners used jam jars to drink from and they made cups from treacle tins to take to work. This village had been designated a 'Category D village' by the county council. 'D' stood for doomed for demolition. There was no hope for its future and there was to be no new building. But the council in their offices underestimated the spirit of the people. This was a community that refused to die. Amid signs of decay and death they would rise again and now the area is growing and thriving once more.

John also took me to Escomb Church with its little round churchyard. This is one of three completely Anglo-Saxon churches in the country. It was built with stones from the nearby Roman camp of Binchester. Into one of the walls is set a stone marking the Sixth Legion. This church was built in about 670. I was deeply moved by leading worship where it had gone on for almost 1,300 years. On the floor was a tomb made from 'Frosterley marble' containing fossilized coral from 325 million years ago. It took me back to the time in the mine when I looked upon the fossils. I gave thanks for the wonders of creation. As this was known as 'Edicum', of the 'Valley of Edi', I could not help but think of one of my favourite Rudyard Kipling poems:

Eddi's service

687 AD

Eddi, priest of St Wilfrid
In his chapel at Manhood End,
Ordered a midnight service
For such as cared to attend.

But the Saxons were keeping Christmas,
And the night was stormy as well.
Nobody came to service,
Though Eddi rang the bell.

'Wicked weather for walking,'
Said Eddi of Manhood End.
'But I must go on with the service
For such as care to attend.'

The altar-lamps were lighted, –
An old marsh-donkey came,
Bold as a guest invited,
And stared at the guttering flame.

The storm beat on at the windows,
The water splashed on the floor,
And a wet, yoke-weary bullock
Pushed in through the open door.

'How do I know what is greatest,
How do I know what is least?
That is My Father's business,'
Said Eddi, Wilfrid's priest.

'But – three are gathered together –
Listen to me and attend.
I bring good news, my brethren!'
Said Eddi of Manhood End.

And he told the Ox of a Manger
And a Stall in Bethlehem,

And he spoke to the Ass of a Rider,
That rode to Jerusalem.

They steamed and dripped in the chancel,
They listened and never stirred,
While, just as though they were Bishops,
Eddi preached them The Word,

Till the gale blew off on the marshes
And the windows showed the day,
And the Ox and the Ass together
Wheeled and clattered away.

And when the Saxons mocked him,
Said Eddi of Manhood End,
'I dare not shut His chapel
On such as care to attend.'

I was privileged to take Evensong in this place and later to celebrate Communion 'for such as care to attend'.

'Mam' Vart – no one called her Alice – made room at her table for Denise who would come from her home in Newcastle most weekends. Denise and I met at Alnwick Castle and were introduced by a prince! It all happened on 23 April 1958. I had returned to my home of Alnwick for a holiday after Easter. With me came Prince Albert. He is a Ghanaian from the Ashanti tribe of which his father was the chief; hence he was a local prince. His full name is Albert Wellington Yamoah Mensa. Albert badly wanted to see inside Alnwick Castle but it was closed to the public. However, as it was a teacher training college for female students, he decided on a course for getting into the castle. He stopped two students on their return walk from collecting celandines for the nature table and asked if they would invite him into the castle. I wanted nothing to do with this! Though they did not know him they were kind enough and foolish enough to invite us both for tea at the weekend. Albert enjoyed his visit and we both enjoyed chatting to these young women. From then I corresponded with Denise and we met up each holiday.

Our letters could hardly have been called 'love letters' as they were more often about something in the religious education essay that Denise was doing or my passing obsession with existential theology and D. H. Lawrence! Yet in this outpouring of our thoughts we were giving each other our attention and ourselves. There was a chipping away at any self-centredness as we wanted to share, to give our life to each other. A sharing of letters and meeting during the holidays had grown more and more into our love for each other. In this growth we were also discovering more of how God loves us all.

Sadly, often in our language, to say, 'I love you' means, 'I want to have you, possess you and own you.' Yet there is a far deeper and more passionate love which is about the giving of oneself to the other. This love is always more respectful and gentle. The people of Spain are known to be passionate people. They make a distinction in what we loosely call love: *Te quiero* means 'I want you', which means the desire, the need, the lusting after, perhaps even the want to control. *Te amo* does not have the same undertones; it is an expression of outgoing love, of the willingness to give and to serve. This word is not used so often because our love is often still very self-centred.

True love moves us out of our self-centredness and opens up for us a whole new way of living and looking at the world. Such love is only possible when we reach out to another with our whole being. It is this sort of love, the outpouring of self, through which God created the world: you were created for love and out of love. The very source of your being is love. In our most fragile moments we know that we are of dust and to dust we shall return but in the depth of our being we know there is more. We are not created out of nothing but out of love, so we will not return to nothing: our journey ends in 'lovers meeting'.

This same love is reflected in the life of Christ. Possibly the best-known text in the New Testament is John 3.16: 'God so loved the world that he gave his only Son, so that everyone who believes in him may not perish but may have eternal life.' Love is seen in the giving of God of his self for you. Some of the words I often meditate upon are from Julian of Norwich:

> Would you know our Lord's meaning in this?
> Learn it well. Love was his meaning.
> Who showed it you? Love.
> What did he show you? Love.
> Why did he show you? For love.
> Hold fast to this, and you shall learn and know more
>   about love, but you will never need to know or
>   understand about anything else for ever and ever.
> Thus did I learn that Love was our Lord's meaning.
> (Julian of Norwich, *Enfolded in Love*,
> Darton, Longman & Todd, 1980, p. 59)

Yet the depth of these words can only be understood once we know we are loved and are able to give ourselves in love. This is something that is not learnt in books but is learnt in relationships with each other and in our relationship with God.

Denise taught in Newcastle so we could only meet up at weekends or in school holidays. Yet by the May time we decided it would be better if we were married and Denise could then teach at a school near West Auckland. We were married in Newcastle in the new year, not long after I was ordained priest. We moved into a small rented house. Denise got a teaching post at Evenwood. Much of the area had suffered from the Depression and never fully recovered. Many families were quite poor, but here were some wonderful children. Children and adults respond well to knowing they are loved and that someone cares for them. In our own growing together in love we were able to reach out in love to others. We were learning to give our undivided attention and our time to all who called upon us or who we worked with.

83

During the time at West Auckland two deaths influenced me greatly. The first was a very pretty young woman dying of leukaemia. For some reason she was often on her own and I went to visit her and to pray with her. All the time I was aware of how unjust and unfair this life can be. But I also sought to know that God is always with us even in our doubt and in our suffering. This was the first time I was present when someone was dying. Outside it was cold and snowing. Inside was warm and comfortable but here a life was fading away. The young woman was beyond speaking to me but still clinging to life. I sat in silence, watching her and watching the exquisite snowflakes slip and melt down the window-pane. I wrote in my diary: 'Against the tenuousness of life, and the injustices of the world, I placed the power and love of God, the promise that we "should not perish but have everlasting life".' It was then I began to rejoice in a statement I have used often: for us 'death is a grave matter but it is not fatal'. For us death is conquered, we are free, Christ has won the victory. I also got comfort from John Donne's poem, 'Death be not proude':

> Death be not proude, though some have called thee
> Mighty and dreadfull, for, thou art not soe,
> For, those, whom thou think'st, thou dost overthrow,
> Die not, poore death, nor yet canst thou kill me.
> From rest and sleepe, which but thy pictures bee,
> Much pleasure, then from thee, much more must flow,
> And soonest our best men with thee doe goe,
> Rest of their bones, and soules deliverie.
> Thou art slave to Fate, Chance, kings, and desperate men,
> And dost with poyson, warre, and sicknesse dwell,
> And poppie, or charmes can make us sleepe as well,
> And better than thy stroake; why swell'st thou then?
> One short sleepe past, wee wake eternally,
> And death shall be no more; death, thou shalt die.

The other person was an elderly lady who was near to dying. I, a young curate, arrogantly was prepared to 'take God' and to bring some peace to this lady. When I entered her room she quietly asked me to sit down. She said, 'Let us say some psalms together.' There were no books but fortunately I had been saying the psalms for a few years by then. We said them verse and verse about as she chose her favourites. After a few psalms she seemed to enter into a deep restfulness and quietly asked for a blessing. I gave the blessing with tears in my eyes. I foolishly had thought I was taking God to her and discovered he had been there long before me! The peace within that room was something to be felt. I had been privileged to be there and I had received a blessing. Once again I learnt the importance of knowing prayers that you love off by heart. Then in a time of trouble or dryness they can be a great strength. I know my mother said the Psalter through each month during the long time she was ill. When my mother died my sister 'inherited' her prayer book and continued with the psalm-saying for many years until her death.

Though I like much of *Common Worship*, the new prayer book for the Church of England, I feel that the recitation of certain psalms every day has been weakened by the pick-and-mix attitude. It is a great pity we do not stay with psalms and canticles.

After over three years at West Auckland we moved across the diocese to what was then West Hartlepool and the parish of St James. This parish was on the large new housing area of Owton Manor. The church had arrived almost as an afterthought and was in one corner of this sprawling estate. In a sense it was built too late and not central enough. Before it arrived people had got used to doing without it. There was a great deal of poverty in the area and a very high level of unemployment. So, there was a necessity to show that someone would care for these people and help them as much as possible in their need.

We had a large Sunday school at St James's. Denise taught and helped to train the six teachers of the infants and younger juniors. There was a man and his helper that taught the older children. There were about 100 children on the books. However, I felt that the top end of the estate was not being looked after by this. With a lay-reader friend we decided to open up a Sunday school in a local school. We gave it good publicity and hoped for results. When we arrived, not only was there a queue to get into the school hall, but also they cheered our arrival. I still wonder what they thought they were going to get. There were well over 400 children! Our resources and our abilities were not up to the task in hand. Much of the time was spent in crowd control. After the second week the numbers had dropped dramatically and we were left with around 100. Like all human beings, many of these children wanted someone to give them attention and to show them they were important in their own right.

Once a week I used to spend a day or an afternoon in a local psychiatric hospital. My primary aim was to visit people from the parish. I met a good few people that I knew and over weeks of visiting I got to know many more. Some of the people received few visitors and they looked forward to anyone calling whom they thought they knew. I realized that many lonely and shy people found the ward a giver of security and where they could get a little attention. It is amazing how many people there are that feel deprived of love and understanding and need to know that someone somewhere cares for them. Often a prolonged stay on the ward was like being given a sense of sanctuary, a 'blanket' that they become afraid to do without. There was a great need to encourage people to extend themselves and to learn to trust the world beyond the ward, tough though it might be. They needed to be able to live without the prop of the ward and the nurses, but with the knowledge that such a support team was there and ready to help.

As people, we all need the support of others in our lives. Ideally it should come from our family and friends, from teachers and people within our community. We all need to be affirmed in our abilities and encouraged when we have failed; we need to know that we are loved whatever state we are in. Unfortunately so many people lack this early love and encouragement and they become afraid to venture, sometimes afraid to go out or to move on. Too often people receive criticism or cautionary advice when they should be encouraged to adventure. The timid suffer in particular. Many are caught between the dream of venturing and the fear of making mistakes and being rejected or criticized. So they do not venture but live in what has been called 'shadowland'.

I discovered many a lovely person who was said to be having a 'breakdown'. These were not inadequate people or deficient in any way; rather they had come to a new turning in their lives and were finding it difficult to face. Sometimes it was a high-powered business person, who was a workaholic and needed to learn how to rest. This was not so much a breakdown as a suffering from physical and emotional exhaustion. To learn to be still and to meditate would greatly help such a person in his or her life. It is important to know that we cannot live in our own strength alone.

There was a young woman who had been offered a new and high-powered job and who had shrunk away at the thought. I explored with her the idea that 'breakdown' was often the refusal or the inability to accept our place in a moving world. Often it was not a breakdown but a clampdown on new feelings and experiences. This arose from a desire to live in the past and often under the false idea that the past was better. It was a refusal to change and to be changed. Time and again you hear people say, 'We have not done it that way and we are not going to start now.' Not only people, but also nations, institutions, businesses and churches suffer from clampdown.

We need to learn when things are no longer useable. I kept an old lawnmower for years. I took it to bits every time it broke down. I spent hours tinkering with the engine. I refused to acknowledge it needed renewing. I wasted hours and caused myself much frustration before the mower finally packed up; if I had got rid of it years before I would have been far better off. I know that none of us are free from clampdown in some areas of our lives and this can use up so much energy without us even noticing. We need to know when we have outgrown certain jobs or attitudes, or even modes of dress. We need to be able to change and to allow ourselves to be changed. In this ever-changing world, we all need to be encouraged and know we have a support system before we can launch ourselves into the new.

The more I heard of breakdowns the more I wanted to say they were really more often a breakthrough that we were refusing. The events of life are often calling upon us to change, and to improve our lot. Through fear of the unknown, through an attachment to what has been, we are unable to move on. Often our past vibrates too strongly in the present. We can spend a good deal of life being unwilling to let go of it; what has been is strong and often prevents us from moving forward. The old life clings tightly around us. I would like everyone to have the experience of the hymn writer John Keble who wrote:

> New every morning is the love
> our wakening and uprising prove;
> through sleep and darkness safely brought,
> restored to life and power and thought.
>
> New mercies, each returning day,
> hover around us while we pray;
> new perils past, new sins forgiven,
> new thoughts of God, new hopes of heaven.
> (*The English Hymnal* 260)

If only it were so easy, but there is a lot of untested truth there. Now almost every day from *Common Worship: Daily Prayer* I like to pray:

> As we rejoice in the gift of this new day,
> so may the light of your presence, O God,
> set our hearts on fire with love for you:
> (*here I add 'for each other, and for the world'*)
> now and for ever.

On my final visits to the hospital, I received a wonderful compliment from a woman who suffered from schizophrenia. I had spent a lot of time with her over the months and she said to me: 'What I really like about you, you are just like us.' I am glad that she was able to recognize our common humanity and that I could easily have also been admitted!

Throughout my time in Hartlepool, I realized more and more the need for simpler and memorable prayers that people could learn. I wanted to find a way of praying that met the needs of the people and left them with resources they could easily use in time of need. I felt the Book of Common Prayer in all its beauty and depth was hardly a beginner's way of praying! I was looking for a way of praying in the home and at work rather than in church and just on Sundays. The old pattern of learning the collect and a psalm did not seem to reach where people were.

It was at this time I delved deeper into *Poems of the Western Highlanders* by G. R. D. McLean, published by SPCK in 1961. These were not prayers said in church buildings but prayers of the Church in daily work: prayers of people rather than the priest. This was a huge nudge in a new direction. One of the first prayers that caught my eye brought me back to the idea of walking with God and God walking with me. Here it is with its preface from the *Carmina Gadelica*:

When the people of the Isles come out in the morning to their tillage, to their fishing, to their farming, or any of their various occupations anywhere, they say a short prayer called 'Ceum na Còrach', 'The Path of Right', 'The Just or True Way.' If the people feel secure from being overseen or overheard they croon, or sing, or intone their morning prayer in a pleasing musical manner. If, however, any person, and especially if a stranger is seen in the way, the people hum the prayer in an inaudible undertone peculiar to themselves, like the soft murmur of the everlasting murmuring sea, or like the far-distant eerie sighing of the wind among trees, or like the muffled cadence of far-away waters, rising and falling upon the fitful autumn wind.

> My walk this day with God,
> My walk this day with Christ,
> My walk this day with Spirit,
> The Threefold all-kindly:
> Ho ! ho ! ho! the Threefold all-kindly.
> (*Carmina Gadelica* III, p. 49)

What a wonderful way of affirming the day! How wonderful it would be to encourage people to pray again like this once again. This is not just an expression of being with God but an actual rejoicing in his presence. Those who 'come into his presence with thanksgiving' lighten their day and their hearts. We discover the relief of not being on our own but much more we find that we are loved by God and upheld by him. This in its turn helps us to relax and so improves our countenance, not only how we look at things but how we look!

There is a need to remind ourselves of the presence of God throughout the day. Prayer does not make God come to us for God is ever-present. Prayer tunes our eyes, our minds, our hearts to the very Presence in which we live and move and have our being.

Our faith is strengthened by little darts of thanksgiving or love directed at God: by affirming, 'You, Lord, are here: your Spirit is with us.' Some like to make the sign of the cross and say, 'In the name of the Father, and of the Son, and of the Holy

Spirit'. This was what was done for each of us at our baptism. The immersion in water was to be a sign of our immersion in the presence and love of God. The latter is far more important than the sign. In doing it we fulfil our Lord's command at the end of St Matthew's Gospel: 'make disciples of all nations, baptizing them in the name of the Father and of the Son and of the Holy Spirit'. To 'baptize' means to 'immerse'. We are called to immerse ourselves and other people in the 'name'; that is in the presence, in the power, in love and in the peace of God. Not a duty but a privilege and a joy, by our own example more often than by our words.

   The people of the Isles said this prayer as they came to their working place, to the seashore, to the farm or anywhere. They often sang their prayer; it had become a hymn of rejoicing and praise. They were so used to the prayer vibrating in their lives that humming it brought them the same awareness of their walking and working with God. It is only by letting certain ideas resound day by day that they become part of our whole being. The Church of the Isles knew the value of 'recital theology', of using words and prayers over and over until they resonated in the depths of their being.

There is a great need to learn prayers by heart, that is, in worship rather than by rote. Prayers are more about our heart being in tune with God than with learning words.

Too often we confine our prayers and our God to a church or chapel. We are in the danger of giving the impression that God is to be found in that building alone or that he can be met only within the service of Holy Communion. There is a danger of suggesting that God is more concerned about our church than he is about the world which he loves. We need to learn to show that God is concerned with, is present in, all of life. He is there when we travel to work, in the office, in the shop, when we are depressed or frustrated. He is present in our joys and celebrations. Even when we forget or ignore him he is still with us. Our faith is not a set of rules laid down but rather an entering into an exciting relationship with the living God who is with us at all times and in all places.

At every moment God seeks entry into your heart. He gives you the opportunity to be part of his kingdom. You are offered the opportunity to live in the kingdom of light, the very kingdom of God, or to go your own way and walk on still in the darkness. Why do you not choose? Why not leave the darkness and walk in hope? Leave your loneliness and learn to walk with God. Here is a challenge for you to take up from Brother Lawrence:

> One way to recall easily the mind in the time of prayer, and preserve it more in rest, is not to let it wander too far at other times. You should keep it strictly in the Presence of God, and being accustomed to think of him often from time to time, you will find it easy to keep your mind calm at the time of prayer, or at least recall it from its wanderings.
>
> Brother Lawrence, *The Practice of the Presence of God*,
> H. R. Allenson, 1906, p. 47)

Such ideas were forever in our minds and I hope in our actions as we sought to share in the life of the people of Owton Manor. Denise and I both loved working there but after over three years we had a feeling that it was time to move on. Once again there was this feeling that it was time for change and we should be facing new challenges.

We were looking forward to having a parish in which to exercise some of our own ideas in ministry after my five years of training and seven years of serving as a curate.

Thought

> For our lives to be fully human, we have to be persons-in-relation – persons who relate 'rightly' to God, to our neighbours, to ourselves and to the cosmos. We cannot relate rightly to God unless we relate rightly to our neighbour. For human

relationships to be life-giving, there is need to recognize the other's human worth and dignity, there is need for mutual respect and reciprocity . . .

Life is our most precious gift from God and we are called to make it most truly human. Neither a subhuman life, nor one that is simply passive, is a fully human life. The Hebrew conception of life is always movement and enjoyment. The evangelist John speaks of eternal life as the true life. But to John, eternal life is not the future resurrected life of believers; it is a life that we already presently enjoy in our earthly existence. Eternal life begins now when we live out Jesus' words of enduring life: 'Love one another'. Our life is one, so there is no division between physical life and spiritual life, between our life of food and drink and our life of relationship to God and neighbour.

(Virginia Fabella, 'Symbols of John's Resurrection
Scene: Reflections on the Garden and Mary Magdalene'
in Lee Oo Chung *et al.*, eds, *Women of Courage: Asian Women
Reading the Bible*, AWRC, 1992, pp. 188–9)

An exercise of prayer using PACTS

Pause in the presence   Be still and know God is with you. That God seeks to have a relationship with you. Turn your attention to God. Enjoy his presence.

Adore   God loves you. Give your love to God who created you out of love and for love.

Confess   Where you have erred and strayed from his way, and turn again to God.

Thank   God for all that he has given to you and his wonder-full creation.

Supplicate   Speak to him on behalf of others and for your own needs. Share with God the relationships you have with your loved ones, your neighbours and with the cosmos. Rejoice that God is with you all and loves all.

Pray

Lord, make me an instrument of your peace.
Where there is hatred, let me sow love;
where there is injury, pardon;
where there is doubt, faith;
where there is despair, hope;
where there is darkness, light;
and where there is sadness, joy.

O Divine Master, grant that I may not so much seek
to be consoled as to console;
to be understood as to understand;
to be loved as to love.
For it is in giving that we receive;
it is in pardoning that we are pardoned;
and it is in dying that we are born to eternal life. Amen.

A homecoming

Cedd chose a site for the monastery among some high and remote hills, which seemed more suitable for the dens of robbers and haunts of wild beasts, than for human habitation. His purpose was to fulfil the prophecy of Isaiah: 'In the habitation of dragons, where each lay shall be grass and rushes', so that the fruits of good works might spring up where formerly lived only wild beasts, or men who lived like the beasts.

(Bede, *A History of the English Church and People*, Book III:23, trans. Leo Sherley-Price, Penguin, 1955)

It was time to move on. I had worked in Owton Manor for three and a half years. Denise and I wanted to have the responsibility of looking after somewhere on our own. We decided that our August holiday would be in north Northumberland and that we would look around with the idea of returning there. We booked our holiday and our plans were made.

The week before going two things happened. It was announced on the radio that foot-and-mouth disease was suspected among the sheep in Northumberland. Glendale and Glanton Agricultural Shows were cancelled. The movement of sheep was restricted. Yet the disease continued to spread with suspected outbreaks at Wandylaw near Chillingham and also in Seahouses and Bamburgh. It was suggested that visitors should not come to these areas. The very area we had planned for holidays became a no-go area.

Then three days before the holidays, as I was on my way to visit someone, the local butcher's van ran into the side of my car. Not much damage but there was the need to go to the nearby garage. I moaned to the garage owner that my holiday was likely in ruins as well as my car damaged. His response was, 'Why not borrow my cottage in Castleton in the Cleveland Hills? It is empty next week but you will need to be out by the Saturday.' I went home and told Denise and it was agreed that it was a marvellous offer.

We had a wonderful week and decided to stay until the Sunday as we had that day off. We stayed in the Fox and Hounds at Ainthorpe. Maybe not a wise choice as Danby had just won the cricket cup and they were celebrating there. Our bedroom was directly above the bar and no soundproofing. The scene below was of great merriment and noise. Above we got very little sleep until about three in the morning when it went silent. Little did we think we were being nudged in a new direction.

The next morning we decided to go to Danby Church which is over a mile from the village and set in a beautiful dale. On the way we passed the vicarage and looking through the gates at this grand house Denise said, 'Let us live there and I could do cream teas!' There was apparently no thought of really coming or of doing cream teas. After the service and before the blessing the vicar asked the congregation if they would stay behind as he had an announcement to make. He told us all he had accepted another post and that he hoped that God would send someone soon. Denise and I did not speak to each other for quite a while. Could we really come to this place? I rang the vicar and asked to see him. He explained that Danby had a private patron, Lord Downe, who lived at Wykeham Abbey, near Scarborough. He gave me the address and after some more thought I contacted him a week later.

Lord Downe invited me to come and see him. I approached his large house with some anxiety and was met by Lady Diana Downe. She apologized for her husband not being present but he was down in the boiler house seeing to a minor repair. This fact relaxed me no end and even more so when Lord Downe appeared with oily hands to greet me. This was a lord incarnate. To cut a long story short, after seeing two more candidates sent by the Archbishop of York, Lord Downe offered me the living.

Now we would move from our modest council house to a vicarage with five bedrooms, plus three 'servant rooms' in the attics, a wonderful farmhouse kitchen, as well as dining room, study, living room, dairy and stables for six horses, all within about half an acre of land and a little woodland. Was such a place not too big for us? All of our furniture would have gone into one room. What had we done? The vicarage itself was a mile from the nearest church and as far from any village. This was far more remote than the Brontës' vicarage at Haworth, and even more remote than the place that inspired *Wuthering Heights*. A friend who heard we had accepted the living sent me a quotation from *Forty Years in a Moorland Parish*: 'Going to see yon place! Why, Danby was not found when they sent Bonaparte to St Helena; or else they never would have taken the trouble to send him all the way there.' These were words said by a friend to Canon Atkinson on his going to look at Danby in 1848. Canon Atkinson was Vicar of Danby from 1848 until his death in 1901, ministering in that one parish for 53 years. The present vicarage had been built for his arrival in 1848.

There were three railway stations, three Anglican churches and three Methodist chapels in the parish. For the Anglicans there was the ancient church of St Hilda set in the middle of Danby Dale and well over a mile from any village. Then there was the beautiful 'arts and crafts' church of St Michael and St George at Castleton whose pews were of adze oak. Nearly all the golden oak woodwork in this church was by the master craftsman Thompson of Kilburn and had his mouse carved on to many pieces. The third church, furthest from the vicarage, was St Peter's, Commondale, built from brick manufactured in the village. This village was thought to have got its name from Colman, the third bishop of Lindisfarne, who was present at the Synod of Whitby in 664. Travelling to this little church for 8.00 a.m. on a snowy winter's morning was often a great adventure. As I have always loved the moors it was a great delight for me to travel across them and to enjoy the sights and sounds of each journey.

There was a sense that we had arrived in a world that was passing away. But we had time to enjoy the old characters and ways for a while. I learnt to use a lye, the Yorkshire word for a scythe. This was so that I could be part of the team that scythed Danby churchyard. By tradition we were paid for this in liquid refreshment. The churchwardens provided us with bottles of beer. It was all Thomas Hardy-like as we lay with our backs to the church wall and drank ale. Though it was not all romantic for it was also a time of blistered hands and aching limbs. One of the scythe men was able to cut the grass fit for a bowling green. This man had helped to take Jerusalem in 1917 having ridden on horseback while being fired on by machine guns. Before entering Jerusalem on 11 December, Sir Edmund Allenby dismounted and, together with his officers, entered the city on foot through the Jaffa Gate out of his great respect for the status of Jerusalem as the Holy City. The same scythe man told me the sad tale that he married his wife for her money and discovered that she had married him for his money. Neither of them had any! Another of the scythe men was the last man to use a flail in the area. In time the scythe men were replaced by various mechanical grass cutters and now the work is contracted out. It is cut far more easily now but a way of fellowship and sharing is lost.

It was not long before Denise started to keep sheep. She became a member of the Wool Marketing Board, which was responsible for collecting the fleeces once a year. Sometimes we sheared our own sheep; we both could do it. But it was always a joy when a local farmer came and did this for us. Not for the ease but for the pleasure of his company. Once or twice we helped in dipping and clipping of sheep at a neighbouring farm. We were soon very much part of the community and really at home on the moors.

Each year on the second Sunday after Easter we held a special service in Castleton Church. This, according to the Book of Common Prayer, was 'Good Shepherd Sunday'. As many still worked as shepherds or kept a few sheep we had a 'Blessing of the Lambs' service. It was a joy to see how many pet lambs would be brought, some walked in following their 'little shepherd'. Others came in on a lead like a dog and yet others were carried. The first lamb Denise ever reared was given to her by a local farmer. It was a runt, the weak one of three lambs. In fact it was such a small creature that the farmer came with another one the next day. He said this was to keep it company and as an aside, 'I thought the first one might not survive.' Denise brought the little runt of a lamb in a shoe box to be blessed. We decided that we would call him Hercules. With a name like that he could hardly stay a runt! In fact he grew to be a great ram and fathered many lambs in the years we were at Danby. We learnt much about sheep and shepherds. We learnt that the runts and the no-hopers are cared for as well as the rest. We discovered what it was like to search for a lost sheep.

A friend of mine who is an artist painted Jesus carrying on his shoulders not a lamb but an old wayward sheep. It had lost half of its fleece and looked decidedly tatty: it was not an object of beauty. He depicted Jesus as weighed down by the sheep and with scratched and dirty hands. When I asked him about this painting he said that we too often portray Jesus with a nice cuddly lamb.

Lambs do not often stray from their mothers; they stay close and under her protection. I wanted to show an old awkward ewe that had a tendency to break through fences and cause trouble with neighbours. The sort that some farmers would feel like sending to the butcher's!

I knew exactly what he meant and I felt he well portrayed how far God will go to find us and in his love seek to bring us home. It was this awareness I wanted to share with my neighbours. Such good news cannot be kept to one's self; it is meant for sharing.

One winter's day I had arranged to take Communion to an outlying farm. The snow was deep on the ground, the temperature well below zero. I had to leave my car on the tarmac road about 400 metres from the farm. I trudged through snow to the farm called Huckaback. When I arrived the man of the house was trying to repair his car. The son was outside doing something else. But I had been seen and they came into the kitchen of the farmhouse. Here was a blazing fire. Ana had laid out a starched linen cloth, which she had crocheted, on one area of their dining table. There were still other things on this table but this space was for us to invite the ever-present God into our lives. Jim, the father, washed his oil-stained hands before we started. We kept a silence for awhile and then celebrated the mystery of Christmas and the 'Word made flesh'. The Christ was received and welcomed by all, including the oil-stained hands of Jim. We placed our lives in the love of God and rejoiced in the mystery of his presence. There was an awareness of Common Union with him who was born in a stable. I left that farm giving thanks for the wonder of how the Christ, born in a stable, comes to us and is ever ready to help us.

On another occasion of a house Communion, I was in a small group of newly built houses for the elderly of the area. Gathered there and waiting for my arrival were: a couple retired from farming, a teacher, a widow of a clergyman and an elderly lady who had been in the church choir for over 65 years. As I celebrated I looked out on the rest of the new housing. I took the bread and broke it, saying, 'This is my body which is broken for you.' At that very moment the door of the house opposite opened. Looking through the two fragments of bread held before me I saw a man carried out on a stretcher. He was not with us making Communion, he never did make his Communion, but we knew the words were for him. The Christ broken on the cross was offered for us all. He gives himself to all of us. It may not have been part of the liturgy, but we held the old farmer before our eyes and in our hearts and I said 'and he is broken for you' mentioning the farmer's name.

I was becoming more and more aware that all Communions are an expression of the one communion we have with God. We are all at all times and in all places in common union with our God. We cannot come to communion for we are in communion. Yet we have the power to ignore this or even deny this. If we wander away from our relationship with God, through our actions and through neglect, if we on our side 'break' our communion, then we cannot hope to be suddenly aware of a deep communion in our Sunday worship. Communion is something we all should enjoy and rejoice in every day.

There is a great need to practise the presence of God: to affirm that God is with us. To rejoice that in him we live and move and have our being. To help us to affirm this I wrote the following prayer that we sometimes used at the beginning of a confirmation class or a study group or an act of worship.

> The Lord is here.
> *Amen.*
> His Spirit is with you.
> *And also with you.*
>
> The Father is here.
> *Amen.*

The Creator is with you
And also with you.

Jesus is here.
Amen.
The Saviour is with you.
And also with you.

The Spirit is here.
Amen.
The Strengthener be with you.
And also with you.

The Trinity is here
Amen.
The Holy Three is all about you.
And also with you.

During my time at Danby I decided there was a need within the Church for a much simpler approach to prayer than the *Book of Common Prayer.* I thought what was needed were more prayers that people could easily say in their homes and in their places of work. I love the Book of Common Prayer and the regular use of the Psalms but I felt there was a need for more earthy, workday prayers. I was looking for homely prayers, prayers of the people at home and at work rather than 'church' prayers. I wanted prayers they could recite easily and would relate to their surroundings. For a few years I had been using and experimenting with forms of Celtic prayer as found in the *Carmina Gadelica*. At the time I was using *Poems of the Western Highlanders* by G. R. D. McLean. I started to use some of the prayers from this book in a confirmation class and in a study group. We had a Lent course on reading some of these prayers and then creating our own. We devised a very informal creed for this occasion where everyone in turn had to add a word or short statement to the second line and then start off the opening line again, when we would all clap twice before the next person took up the theme:

> O God, I believe that you are (clap, clap)
> The eternal father of . . .

This would end, when all had had an opportunity of adding something, with the words:

> O God, I believe that you are
> here and with us now.

Another prayer we developed was the 'Caim', which is the Celtic word for an encircling prayer. I taught that this prayer is often easily understood as 'We are in God and God is in us'. The other way I described it was 'A prayer of seven directions: God before me, God behind me, God on my right and on my left, God above me, God beneath me'. I would then stop and point out that this prayers shows that we are encircled by God. It was never long before someone said, 'But that is only six directions.' I would then say, 'The six directions tell us that God is greater than we are and is all about us wherever we go. Only after we experience the greatness of God can we truly rejoice in the last direction that God is in us.'

The teenagers and the confirmation class would often lead the intercessions at Evensong on a Sunday; obviously, only after they had been prepared and prayed the prayers during the week. One of the young boys who learnt a simple prayer deeply moved the congregation when he prayed in very free manner:

> You, Lord, are in my home.
> You, Lord, are in my work.
> You, Lord, are in my heart.
> You, Lord, are in my life.
> You, Lord, are here and with us now
> You Lord are.
> You Lord
> You.

He told us how he had been using this prayer every day at home and at work among the sheep. It reminded me of St Patrick when he was a slave in Ireland and tells us in his *Confessions*: 'After I came to Ireland – and tend sheep, every day, I often prayed in the daytime . . . up to a hundred prayers and in the night nearly as many.' Patrick would be about the same age as this young shepherd boy leading our prayers.

In 1980 the Deanery of Whitby celebrated the thirteenth centenary of St Hilda's death with a service in the ruins of Whitby Abbey, which she founded. I was at Whitby too for the first meeting of the Whitby Deanery Synod, and couldn't resist asking to have the minutes of the previous Synod read. The secretary rose to the bait and said there were none, but in fact there is quite a good set of minutes in Bede's *History of the English Church and People* dating from 664! Throughout the 1980s I studied and taught about Hilda, Aidan, Cuthbert, Patrick and many other of the Celtic saints.

I became particularly interested in Celtic spirituality and especially the prayers from Celtic lands. This meant that the confirmation class of young teenagers and the adults who attended a Lent course were presented with new ideas of praying. We spent the Lent of 1984 doing simple Celtic drawings and looking at Celtic knotwork. We explored the idea that the knotwork with its pattern of over and under could be a way of looking at the joys and sorrows of life, the good times and the bad times. In all these rises and falls of life we survived because we were still here. In silence we gave thanks to God for his presence at all times. Then we noticed the knotwork is endless: it is without beginning or end, a sign that life is eternal. We created prayers in the Celtic tradition. This was not to go back in time but to be enriched by a simple way of praying. We were creating our own prayers and making prayers we could use in our daily lives. I was writing a prayer a day and encouraged others to do the same. It is a good idea to keep a prayer diary.

Due to the suggestion of a friend, I sent a batch of my prayers along with drawings from some of the people of the parish to SPCK and to our amazement and joy they were accepted. My first book, *The Edge of Glory*, was born. It was just as it was accepted that I went to visit a friend in the parish who was an artist and he had produced a wonderful lino print of Holy Island. It was just what I was looking for and it made a splendid cover to my first book.

I started to teach about Celtic prayer and spirituality to various groups and churches. The parish hosted a few days for a group from the United Society for the Propagation of the Gospel and I did much of the teaching. At a similar event on 31 August 1987, I was on Holy Island sharing in a study of Celtic spirituality and celebrating the life of Aidan. Late that evening, I felt I was seeking something; or something or Someone was seeking me. As usual this was rather vague. This was the anniversary of the night in 651 that Aidan died at Bamburgh and the same night Cuthbert saw angels descending to the earth and taking a holy soul up to heaven. The next day Cuthbert heard that Aidan had died. He saw this as a sign and offered himself to the monastery of Melrose. On that same night 1,300 years later, I felt that again I was being called to do something new. What I did not know.

I walked out of the retreat house on Holy Island and made my way into the dark. I asked two other residents at the retreat house to come with me. If something happened I needed a witness or two. Going into the dark was a symbol of where I stood. People often tell me that God has told them what to do. I always seem to struggle to discover his will. As soon as we left the few streetlights I saw a shooting star, then another and another. After foolishly counting them, up nearly to a hundred, I gave up. I wanted to ask, did Cuthbert see stars or angels? I knew the answer was 'Yes', though he might have seen it differently! The question is not about 'either or' for it demands an answer of 'both and more'. We need not choose between stars and angels but we need to keep ourselves alert to the greater potential that is ever being presented to us through the material world. You might decide the night was full of stars and that is beautiful enough. I decided that once again God was calling me to do something – but what?

Synchronicity is a strange thing. I thought of the words of Archbishop William Temple, 'When I pray coincidences happen: when I do not pray they do not happen.' Though I actually believe that wonderful coincidences happen all the time to those who have their eyes, ears and hearts open to the Almighty. Was it a nudge to send me in a new direction? It certainly moved me, but I did not know any definite call from it.

In 1989 I was made a canon of York, in the minster that is on the site where Paulinus baptized Hilda and Edwin, where Chad was bishop and Wilfrid built a stone church. It was here that Archbishop Theodore consecrated Cuthbert as bishop in front of King Egfrith on Easter Day in 685. Once again a 'cloud of witnesses' surrounded me. Here was the history of the Church in England all about me and I was a living part of it. No wonder I felt overawed when made 'canon of York and prebend of Botevant' and was led to my own stall within the minster. When I asked where Botevant was I was told that no one really knows; it was probably on the coast somewhere and had fallen into the sea. I was likely made the prebend of a lost community of an area of land under the sea. Its very name Botevant probably meant 'Bote', that is 'booty' or 'profit', and 'vant' meaning 'want', so it was 'of little profit'.

Perhaps this was reflected in my payment for being a canon: I was given a once-off payment of one bread bun! No one can say that the Church is not quaint at times or that it lacks a sense of humour. I took my bread bun home, baked it until it was hard and then varnished it. So I am still the possessor of a 20-year-old bread bun!

Among earlier prebends of Botevant in the sixteenth century was William Turner, the father of English botany, who was a fellow Northumbrian coming from Morpeth, and James Basset, who was in a plot to murder Elizabeth I.

Denise and I were greatly enriched by the life we lived on the North Yorkshire Moors. We had built up many friends and deep relationships. But from the mid-1980s there was a feeling that it was maybe time to move on. Not only to allow someone else the delights of the parish of Danby but also that we might not become too settled and stop growing. Yet unless something was for us especially to do we could not see any reason for uprooting. We both firmly believed that people needed to be offered some stability in an ever-changing world. If clergy were forever on the move, how could they offer stability? We had been in Danby long enough to be confirming and marrying children that we had baptized. We felt part of a large family.

Thought

Love all God's creation, the whole and every grain of sand of it. Love every leaf, every ray of God's light. Love the animals, love the plants, love everything. If you love everything, you will perceive the divine mystery in things. Once you perceive it, you will begin to comprehend it better every day. And you will come at last to love the whole world with an all-embracing love.

(Fyodor M. Dostoyevsky, *The Brothers Karamazov*, Barnes & Noble Classics, New York, 2004, pp. 293–4)

Exercise with Celtic knotwork

Look at the pattern of Celtic knotwork on page x.

Place your finger on the pattern and trace around it, over each rise and going under.

Look at your life as you do this. Give thanks for times when you experience joy and growth on each rise. You may like to affirm, 'I arise today.'

At each going under of the pattern look at times of sorrow, loss or sin. You may like to pray, 'Lord, have mercy.'

Know that in all the rises and falls God is ever-present. In all the open and in all the hidden things of your life God is with you.

No matter what has happened in the past, though it has shaped your personality, know that you are still alive and still in the love of God.

Finally look at the whole pattern and notice the pattern is endless. It is a symbol that in God life is eternal.

Pray this affirmation

> You, Lord, are in this place, your presence fills it.
> You Lord are in this place.
> You Lord are.
> You Lord.
> You.

Say each line slowly, with meaning, not only on your lips but with your heart. Rejoice in the love and goodness of God.

The Lord is here

> I came to see that there is no space without God: space does not exist apart from God. God is in heaven, in hell and beyond the seas. God lives in everything and enfolds everything. God embraces all that is, and is embraced by the universe: confined to no part within it, he encompasses all that exists.
>
> (Hilary of Poitiers, *On the Trinity*)

The invitation to become the Vicar of Holy Island came as a surprise. I had begun to think, as we had completed 23 years in this one parish, we would spend the rest of our lives there. We were reasonably settled. Yet somewhere at the back of our minds there was something else saying, 'It is time to move on.'

Holy Island is a small island off the Northumbrian coast and near the border with Scotland. The island can be seen from the A1 when you travel north from Belford. It is in an area of outstanding natural beauty and is know for its bird life as well as its saints. As a tidal island the phases of the moon and the tides govern all movements. The tide is never at the same time two days in a row. The movements of residents, pilgrims, fishermen and the wading birds are all controlled each day. Twice in every 24 hours the island is cut off by the North Sea and no one can reach it by road. Bede, who was an early authority on tides, calls the island a demi-isle and writes of it and its tides: 'As the tide ebbs and flows, this place is surrounded twice daily by waves of the sea like an island, and twice, when the sands are dry it becomes again attached to the mainland.'

Walter Scott in his poem *Marmion* writes more romantically of the tide and pilgrims:

The tide did now its flood-mark gain,
And girdled in the Saint's domain:
For with the ebb and flow its style
Varies from continent to isle;
Dry-shod, o'er sands, twice every day,
The pilgrims to the shrine find way;
Twice every day, the waves efface
Of staves and sandall'd feet the trace.
(Walter Scott, *Marmion: A Tale of Flodden Field*,
II.9, London, Cassell, 1904, pp. 39–40)

No one can expect to cross to the island just when they decide to. Tide tables must be consulted to find out when the way is clear. It is of no use to arrive just after the tide has closed or if you need a quick exit from the island at high tide. It must be remembered this is not a stream that is being crossed but the North Sea.

It was the latter part of 1989, when the Bishop of Newcastle telephoned me. He began by saying he had sought permission from my bishop to offer me a parish in the diocese of Newcastle: it was Holy Island. My immediate reaction was, 'No, thank you.' But the bishop asked me to think about it and, if I wanted, to visit it. Denise thought we ought to go and look at it and see if we believed we could work there. I was still hesitant; possibly because I do not look forward to moving. But we decided we ought at least to go and look at the parish and the vicarage. We knew the island a little, though not very well.

The bishop told me of the very small congregation who met regularly. He also spoke of the island being a special place, a place of the saints and also a place of pilgrimage. We had our doubts about it being the place for us and the idea of a saintly place was daunting. Fortunately, I knew that the islanders had a reputation of being very earthy. We came. We looked and we hesitated. We tried to escape the challenge, but it would not let us go. I talked to a friend and he said, 'It is just the sort of place made for you. You can see God's hand at work.' I only wished that I could see. I asked God to guide me but he gave me no clear directions! I loved living on the high North Yorkshire Moors. I was reluctant to move. I was a case of God calls and man stalls. Other people seemed to think it was right, I still had to be convinced. Denise saw it more clearly than I did and she knew we must move on. It took us three months to make our minds up; another three months to serve our notice and to get rid of 23 years of clutter. We found leaving Danby and the farewells very painful. We arrived on Holy Island just after Easter 1990 to look after, to learn from and to share with 150 people, man, woman and child.

When I was inducted to the parish, I was given the key to the church, a stole embroidered with the figures of Aidan and Cuthbert, and a copy of the *Lindisfarne Gospels*. These signs of my inheritance represented a history of more than 1,300 years and reminded me of the great responsibility I faced. This little island has long been regarded not only as a special place but, as Rabbi Lionel Blue put it, the 'holiest place in holy England'. It certainly seems to have more saints per square metre than you can find almost anywhere else.

I was told the key I had been given was the only key to the church yet I already had in my possession a key that fitted the lock. This was a large ancient key, acquired many years ago, which is more than ten inches long and was hand-forged by a blacksmith out of a single piece of metal. One end of the key is shaped like a clover leaf, in a Celtic pattern, to symbolize the Trinity. Quite wonderfully, after having this key for about 20 years, I found when I moved to Lindisfarne that it opened and locked the church door! Keys are often a symbol of authority and power, for they give the holder some control over a building or a treasure. As I held this ancient key, which had waited so long to be used, I felt encouraged to trust in my ability to care for this sacred place.

At the back of the church, before my first Sunday service, I looked at the list of saints, bishops, priors, priests and incumbents who had been given pastoral care of the island. It began with Aidan in 635 and included no fewer than 16 bishops, including Finan, Colman, Eadfrith and Cuthbert. To follow such men (I spotted my name at the very bottom of the list!) and to try and reflect something of their holiness was a truly awesome challenge. A little consolation came with the knowledge that, like the sea around the island, places and people ebb and flow. There were times in the past when the island had been sadly run down and the church neglected and ruinous. Here I would be asked to pray where Aidan had prayed: to pray where prayer had been said for over 1,300 years. I would be expected to exercise pastoral care where Cuthbert had exercised his care, where he had given comfort and solace to those who came to him from afar. People still came here for healing and for forgiveness, for spiritual direction and for new hope.

We had our suspicions, but no one had mentioned the amount of pilgrims coming to the island. Now thousands of people came every year. I would meet pilgrims from all over the world, who had the same love for Aidan and Cuthbert as I had and who wanted to show that God is in their lives. Time and again I would lead services in celebration for the witness of the saints of northern England. The pilgrims would come as individuals, as small groups or occasionally three or four thousand at a time. Nearly all groups expected some spiritual input. All had to be planned within the limits of the tide being open for the day.

Then there were school groups, many unplanned, who thought they could just use the building. In a year we would deal with about 7,000 children who actually booked in for some teaching. On one horrendous day – I should be able to say glorious – because the weather had stopped school groups doing other things, instead of the 80 to 90 we had booked in, we had over 950 children in three hours.

Obviously the potential for outreach was enormous and only limited by space and human resources. This was certainly not like running a normal parish.

The vicarage would receive endless visitors looking for hope, healing, help or simply hospitality. Some booked, others arrived on the doorstep. You could not immediately tell if someone was merely curious and fancied seeing into your house or whether they were suicidal. Each had to be given time and attention, not to forget your discernment. The doorbell, the telephone and the church bell all demanded attention and often at the same time. There was the odd occasion when we had someone needing attention in each of our downstairs rooms and someone else waiting across at church. We averaged about three visitors a day for every day of the year, and that only counts the ones that took over a quarter of an hour of our time within our home.

The rhythm of daily worship would ensure some balance in this hyperactive existence, though some might not think so as we had a minimum of three services every day, not counting any others for school groups or pilgrims. There were odd days when I was in church for over six hours. Fortunately we were able to build up a team of helpers. There was little time to be proactive as we had too much to react to and it had to be within a single tide. The majority came for only one opening of the tide.

There was a great danger of not having enough time for each other, for ourselves or for the seekers who came to us. Yet this was a greatly rewarding life. We saw the Church alive, exciting and, often, in great numbers. So many people enriched us. As pilgrims shared their journey they often allowed us to share in their insights. We learnt from them new hymns, new modes of worship, deep and meaningful readings, and a great keenness of adventure in the faith. We built up friendships with musicians, artists, crafts people and members of religious communities, all who came and added to the beauty and to the depth of the place. We learnt of humility, perseverance and of tremendous courage. Sometimes we were given a material gift, such as when the group from Selkirk brought us a 'Selkirk Bannock'. The Dean of Trondheim in Norway rang me up and offered to bring me St Olaf's head! I had visions of me standing there and saying, 'Alas, poor Yorick. I knew him well.' Fortunately this latter gift was a small plaster cast and not the real thing. One American group 'paid' me for my talk in peanuts – I wondered if they saw that was its worth!

Some friends thought we were mad in moving. They thought we were off to some rocky outpost set out in the North Sea remote from all activity. Well, the population was tiny. The bishop had said there were only a handful of regular churchgoers and only five children in the school. I did not have the sense to check all the facts. I was soon overawed and overworked by the number of people that came to the door, and to church for services. Every day we had Morning Prayer, Holy Communion and Evening Prayer. This was then increased by pilgrims and school groups coming for worship or for some teaching. Then there were individual pilgrims, seekers, and people wanting guidance or help. There were under 150 residents on the island but it was visited by about a third to half a million people every year.

I wondered how many small villages could cope with this, especially as the crowds were stacked up by the tide. Not all the residents were able to cope with the visitors, as some were employed in fishing and farming and some were elderly. Very few people were dealing with great numbers. The words of Churchill came to mind: 'Never in the field of human conflict was so much owed by so many to so few.' There were not many country churches expected to put up with the flow of visitors like this. Many a day we would have more than the cathedral in Newcastle but without the staffing. In my first year there were well over 140,000 people through the church doors, 7,000 children had some teaching, and over 1,200 people visited the vicarage for over half an hour. Denise often witnessed me going to sleep as I ascended the stairs in the late evening.

A phone call from a very pleasant lady was quite typical. She asked if she could bring a pilgrimage to the island in the summer. I asked the reason for the pilgrimage and she said for peace and to celebrate the saints of Holy Island. When I asked how many would there be she said, 'At the moment about 2,000 plus but it could be nearer 3,000.' Obviously this visit was already underway on their part, whatever I said. This dear lady wondered if I would celebrate the Communion and communicate them! A thousand alarm bells began to ring. Without help how long would it take to communicate over 2,000 people? Obviously it would need to be outside in the ruined priory or some other open space. There would need to be a sound system, and plenty of chalices and ciboria, not to forget all the people that would be needed to help in the communicating of such a crowd. On a more mundane level, there would be need for special arrangements to park up to 60 buses. The police would need to be informed of so many buses coming and going. They would need more toilets than the public ones on the island, so they would have to bring Portaloos. For reasons of safety, they needed a medical presence in the form of St John Ambulance Brigade or something similar. All of this would have to take place within the tides, and had the organizer ever thought of the logistics of this? Added to this there would still be other buses bringing visitors and other people wanting to come to the island and the church on that day.

On another occasion, the phone rang and it was a very clearly spoken English voice asking if a group could come on pilgrimage. 'We are from France and we would like you to say

Mass for us.' More alarm bells. I explained that I was the Anglican vicar and not a Roman Catholic priest. 'We understand, but we would like you to celebrate for us in your church. However there is yet another slight problem, only I speak English, the rest are French-speaking.' Over the next week we planned a form of service with hymns in French, the congregation responses in Latin and the rest in English, with the actions they were all aware of showing what stage we were at in the Mass. The Lord's Prayer I said in English as they said it in French. My short welcome and homily were translated by the one English speaker. They did not warn me that every three people were bringing a flag and these were received into the sanctuary during the first hymn. The whole service was very moving and I received a hug and a kiss on both cheeks from each of the worshippers. Later the same day I led worship for a group of Salvation Army captains and a few other evangelicals. There was certainly a need to be adaptable in the approach to worship and people.

On a typical August day by noon, I had already taken three services and spoken to over 60 American visitors. The church was heaving with people. At this moment it felt more like a supermarket than a place of prayer. I just wanted to escape. At the back of the church sat a busload of Saga pilgrims, obviously a little tired. They were trying to eat their packed lunches without being noticed. In the south aisle a very intelligent man was standing by the facsimile of the *Lindisfarne Gospels* and proclaiming his wisdom. He was speaking in a stage whisper so that all could hear and acknowledge his wisdom. In the north aisle a group of children were sitting on the carpet and making merry sounds. Their chortling showed they were very happy to be where they were. There were at least 150 people just wandering around; most looked rather lost. The main aisle had three mums with buggies. I am convinced that people with buggies – or supermarket trolleys – tend to display their genetic descent from Boudicca! Anyone who stands in the road is in danger of being mown down. Someone stopped me and asked, 'Do you still have services in this church?' When I told him, 'At least three every day', he refused to believe me, saying, 'No one goes to church that often.' I felt I had had enough for one morning. What can be done with such a madding crowd? I wanted to be far from it. With the excuse of lunch, it was time to escape this busy place.

Before I could get to the door, in strode a group of young people. They made straight for the front pews on either side of the main aisle. As there were about 20 of them, they almost filled four pews. After a deep bow to the east, they all knelt except one. This was a pretty young woman who stood with arms raised in prayer. Suddenly, the whole church was silent. The air began to tingle. There was some strange power at work. You could actually feel it. No one in the church dared to move. The children were the first to sense the change and became absolutely still and quiet. The loud speaker ceased from his lecture. The Saga pilgrims stopped eating their sandwiches and bowed their heads. All were being touched by something deep and mysterious. You could actually feel something with your whole being. There was a sense of expectancy in the air. We were waiting for something to happen. After a while, the young woman lowered her arms. The whole group then arose, made a bow and went out. They left a hushed building and people that were aware that something special had just taken place. How long the vibrant silence lasted I could only guess. It must have been at least two or three minutes.

Who were these young folk? What had made them come here and what were they doing in the church? I could not resist following them out and enquiring about their visit. Sadly, I should have been able to guess they were not English. In fact they could not speak English except for one young man. His sentences were slow and thoughtful. 'We are from Slovakia. As Christians, we have a new freedom. To celebrate our new liberty, we sought one of the holiest places we had heard of and came to give thanks to God. Our pilgrimage is one of thanksgiving.' Needless to say, I was deeply moved by the directness and simplicity of his statements. It was the next sentence that caused me much joy and amusement. 'I hope that we did not disturb anyone.' I could only take his hand and say, 'Thank you. I believe that you have disturbed us all by revealing the Presence that is ever with us. God bless you all on your journey.'

I would never see these young people again but what they did on that busy August day would remain with me forever. Without words they had introduced our visitors to the holy and the mysterious. Their faith gave them a confidence, not in themselves but in their God. They rejoiced in his presence and helped others to be more aware of the God in their midst. I am sure they did not need to come to the island to find God, they knew that God was with them. They did not come to proclaim God, yet their very lives and actions said, 'The Lord is here.' The Celtic monks on Holy Island were like this in the sense of who they were, and how they lived spoke more loudly than the mere words they said.

Each year a Roman Catholic school came from Doncaster; their visit was always near Ascension Day. They were a group that would lead the worship and I would speak to them. The teacher that came with them was a gem; he made sure the children understood their faith and enjoyed it. The children would read poems, play instruments, sing and lead prayers. They would also sit in absolute silence before a candle or some image they had created to express the love of God. As the church on the island had the ascension as the theme for its east window we often talked about the ascended yet ever-present Christ. Above the Christ was a cloud with a stylized sun above it. The sun was hidden by the cloud, yet rays of light penetrated through to the disciples below. Although the symbolism was good it looked as if the ascended Christ had a large hat above him or a jelly! I loved to describe this window as 'Jesus of the jelly' to get reactions.

One year the Doncaster children were approached this way and asked what they thought of 'Jesus of the jelly'. One little lad's hand shot up and I could see he was bursting to say something. I invited him to make a comment.

> Do you not know that it is the Shekinah you are talking about?
> The sun behind the cloud is about the hidden glory of God.
> Though we cannot see him God is always present and his glory
> is all about us. We should all learn about the hidden God who
> is always with us. This hidden sun represents God our Father
> and is a very special part of the window.

With this he sat down and puffed out his chest. He had done his job well. There was a beaming smile on the teacher's face and on all of the children's. I knew that I had been set up! Suddenly for the sheer joy of it we were all laughing at this event.

This school group was always well prepared and settled easily into worship. They had discovered something of the glory and grace of God in their lives. For these children prayer and sitting in the presence of God was part of their daily routine at school. It was as vital to them as learning any other subject. In fact their worship often enhanced and enriched the rest of what they were doing and their work enhanced their worship. They were learning that God and his world were not separate and that God could be found through his creation – though he was often well hidden. Even on the cloudiest and darkest days we can say, 'The Lord is here.' In *Hebridean Altars*, Alistair Maclean expresses this well:

> As the rain hides the stars, as the autumn mist hides the hills, as
> the clouds veil the blue of the sky, so the dark happenings of my
> lot hide the shining of Thy face from me. Yet, if I may hold Thy

hand in the darkness, it is enough. Since I know that, though
I may stumble in my going, Thou dost not fall.

(Alistair Maclean, *Hebridean Altars*,
Edinburgh, Moray Press, 1937, p. 70)

The hidden glory of God is always there waiting to be revealed
to those who seek it, to those who seek him. As an exercise
I have often plunged the church into total darkness as symbol
of our world and our life without the presence of God. If it is
in the summer I ask pilgrims to cover their eyes and to keep
them completely closed. We remain in the darkness for a while.
Then I ask them to open them – look at the light or a lighted
candle. The light was there all the time; it was us who had
closed our eyes or turned from it. We had chosen to exclude
the light, and now we had turned to the light. If we were
suddenly thrust into darkness surely we would strive with all
our being to seek the light. In the same way we should seek the
hidden glory of our God.

Teilhard de Chardin expresses that 'The Lord is here' though
hidden from sight:

God who made man that he might seek him – God whom we
try to comprehend by the groping of our lives – that self-same
God is as pervasive and perceptible as the atmosphere in which
we are bathed. He encompasses us on all sides, like the world
itself. What prevents you then, from enfolding him in your arms?
Only one thing: your inability *to see him*.

(Teilhard de Chardin, *Le Milieu Divin*, Fontana, 1975, p. 46)

The presence of God says no one needs to travel far on
pilgrimage. We can find our holy place in our home or nearby.
For some it is not to travel through space but it is to have
a change of heart or mind. For some it is the discovery that
'The Lord is here: his Spirit is with us'. Sometimes our place
of pilgrimage can be presented to us by a friend or loved one.
As an example, one weekday one of the island children was

brought to church, when it was empty, by her father to 'see the King' and to kneel quietly in his presence. Most days he brought her to the communion rail and let her kneel looking up at the window of Christ's ascension. Here she was learning to be quiet, to give her love to the King and to stay with him for a while. She would have made a lovely picture as she knelt at the communion rail with her blonde head looking upwards. There she waited before her God and was sure that he loved her.

She reminded me of the person whom Jean-Baptiste Vianney, the Curé d'Ars, found often kneeling in church. When asked by the Curé what he was doing, he replied, 'I look at him and he looks at me.' It is the ability to be aware of God and his love that will transform our lives. In his instructions to his people the Curé d'Ars wrote:

> My children reflect that a Christian's treasure is not on earth but in heaven. Therefore our thoughts should turn to where our treasure is. Ours is a noble task: that of prayer and love. To pray and to love, that constitutes the greatest possible happiness for us in this life. Prayer is nothing less than union with God ... My children I know your hearts are small, but prayer will enlarge them and make them capable of loving God.
>
> (Jean-Baptiste Vianney, *Catechetical Instructions: Sermons* (4 vols), Lyon, 1883, quoted in *Celebrating the Saints*, Canterbury Press, 1998)

This little lass was one of the fortunate ones, her parents were people of faith and wanted their daughter to know and love God. Her father did not come to church services but he wanted to share with her the faith he had learned. As a father should, he handed on the ability to be still and quiet before God. He sought out times of day when he thought the church would be empty as he preferred the stillness to church services. He would talk to her about the windows and other things in church and then get her to come and kneel for a while before 'the King',

telling her of God's love for her and that she should give her
love to him.

At one weekday Evening Service we had just begun the first
few words when the door opened. We were used to this as
pilgrims often wandered in while we prayed. This time a little
voice shouted out quite clearly, 'David, this is for youoo. This
is for youoo.' Down the aisle this same little girl came repeating
the refrain, 'David, this is for youoo. This is for youoo.' We
stopped our prayers and watched. The little blonde lass came
carrying a large basket of flowers. The congregation of about
a dozen were all beaming, if not chuckling. The service was
halted. The congregation watched and awaited the presenta-
tion. She came, looked at me, and said, 'This is for youoo.' Then
there was just a slight pause. 'And it is for the King.' She trotted
to the sanctuary and placed the flowers at the communion rail.
She knelt for a moment in silence. She turned around, gave
us a wave and then left, skipping her way out of church. By
then, the beaming smiles had turned to watery eyes. With such
simplicity and love the little lass reminded us all why we were
gathered together and whom we sought. We had also come to
kneel before the King and to give ourselves to him. Whatever
would be remembered of that service we would not forget the
little lass and her flowers.

By 1997, my seventh year on the island, I had spoken to over
50,000 children and seen more than a million people through
the church doors. The opportunities for outreach and sharing
in worship seemed to be growing year by year. Many school
groups, church visits and pilgrimages had been booked for the
months ahead, and on one day, the island would be invaded
by at least 60 bus loads of people, from the Church Army, plus
the Third Order of St Francis, and the parish of Guisborough!
I had the challenge of ensuring each group would find a place
of peace and quiet amid the crowds, though I had no doubt
the island would work its usual wonders.

The year 1997 was the fourteenth centenary of the death of St Columba and the beginning of the mission of St Augustine to Britain. I made my way towards the church on Easter Eve. The Northern Cross Pilgrims coming from Carlisle, Hexham and Haddington had walked from their home areas over moor and byroad carrying life-sized crosses. They were joining other pilgrims in church to celebrate Easter. No lights would be put on this Holy Saturday evening: the gathering gloom was a symbol of life without Christ, without God. Darkness filled the church; only those who read the Scriptures or said the prayers offered us a little light. Sometimes as their reading ended we all returned to the darkness. The darkness closed around us, reminding us that we could suddenly be plunged into darkness without or within. In the flickering light we heard promises, promises, promises. But we need far more than promises, we need a Presence. More than words we need a personal relationship. We needed a voice to say, 'The Lord is here'. After what seemed an age of promises, we went out into the night. We began to go downhill on a rocky road that had pitfalls to avoid. I was thankful for the small illumination afforded by the moon and for the clearly visible Hale-Bopp comet (which we would not see again for 2,380 years!) All these things were good symbols of the spiritual journey: we are often in the dark, feeling that life is a bit rough and that we are going downhill. Our eyes were cast downward, watching our step.

Then a corner was turned and we knew someone had been at work in the darkness. There on the shore facing the sea and Cuthbert's Island blazed the flames of a bonfire. Its light reflected in our eyes and on our faces, we could feel its warmth. It was a flame that could engulf us: it needed to be approached with caution. The events of the Easter Garden and the shore of Galilee were breaking into our world, reaching the shore of Lindisfarne, the shores of our lives, and to the shore of eternity. The Light and presence of Christ was breaking through to dispel the darkness of the night. I approached the fire with due respect and caution, knowing I could be burned. In a white alb, wearing the white stole with Aidan and Cuthbert worked upon it, I had to light a large Easter candle from the blaze. Both wax and I melted a little, but I managed on the third attempt as people looked and waited in hope. Now it was the time, a new day dawned. I proclaimed those wonderful words: 'May the Christ risen in glory scatter the darkness from our hearts and minds and from this world. Alleluia! Christ is risen, Alleluia! He is risen indeed, Alleluia!' After a few short prayers, we turned back towards the church singing 'Walk, walk in the light'. At the entrance to the building, everyone lit a candle from the Easter Candle. Light now filled the church, as we prayed that the 'Light of Christ' would fill our lives.

I thought of and gave thanks for all who have passed on the light: Columba, Augustine and especially Aidan, whose statue – with burning torch in hand – stands within the churchyard. Bishop Lightfoot of Durham, when wishing to express the contribution of St Aidan, not only to the northern part of England, but to the wider reaches of this land through those who went out in mission from Lindisfarne, penned a very memorable phrase: 'Augustine was the Apostle of Kent, but Aidan was the Apostle of England.' I was truly thankful that I was able to share in the outreach and praise of the church on Holy Island.

Amid our busyness there was often much joy and laughter as there should be in any Christian community. There were times when we could laugh at ourselves and not take ourselves too seriously. There was one wonderful moment that tickled the islanders' sense of humour. I had been leading some late prayers at the retreat house. In cassock I went home, picked up the church key and invited our Yorkshire terrier to come across with me as I locked the church. It only took about a minute. In that time this little dog had gone under a leaning headstone in pursuit of a rabbit. He was completely out of sight. So I went over and knelt by the gravestone and shouted, 'Will you come out of there!' I had not noticed the two visitors coming around the corner. They saw me, heard me and fled. I never saw them again. The islanders laughed for days.

By 2003 the island had become very much part of our life, but life was moving on. It was time for someone else to bring their insights and energies to the island. We made the very hard decision that it was time to go. We wanted to stay in Northumberland and, after some seeking, found a house in a quiet hamlet. It was on land once given to St Cuthbert, though we did not know that at the time. It just felt like the right place for us. From here we would discover new ventures.

Thought

No man or woman begins to live a full life until they realize they live in the presence of something greater, outside and beyond themselves. Self-consciousness truly means you are standing over against that other than yourself and you cannot be living in the truth. Wonder is at the base of true living, and wonder leads to worship and after that the great other than self; it is yet kin to you, you are one with it.

(G. A. Studdert Kennedy, *The New Man in Christ*, Hodder & Stoughton, 1932, p. 132)

Exercise

Affirm throughout the day that the Lord is with you. Release the words, 'The Lord is here: his Spirit is with us' from being words in church alone to become part of your daily prayers and said throughout the day. Rejoice in the Presence. To help you, you may like to learn the following prayer or devise one of your own.

We need not fear,
His Spirit is with us.

We are surrounded by love,
His Spirit is with us.

The Lord is here

We are immersed in peace,
His Spirit is with us.

We rejoice in hope,
His Spirit is with us.

We travel in faith,
His Spirit is with us.

We live in eternity,
His Spirit is with us.

The Lord is in this place,
His Spirit is with us.
(David Adam, *Tides and Seasons*,
SPCK, 1989, p. 47)

Pray

Awaken us to your glory
Dispel the darkness of night
Destroy the heaviness of heart
Cure the blindness of sight
Heal the deafness of ears
Open the mouth that is dumb
Restore a gentleness of touch
Encourage a sense of adventure
Bring us an awareness of you
Awaken us to your glory.
(David Adam, *Tides and Seasons*,
SPCK, 1989, p. 128)

The world of the other

Do you have a sense of mystery? No generalization can be pressed too hard, but it does seem as if there is a thick sheet of glass placed, not between people of different creeds and cultures, but between those who have a sense of mystery (properly, a religious sense) and those for whom wonder is a luxury they can do without. We can see each other through the glass, but we can't hear each other for we're talking a different language, those with the capacity to see the extraordinary in the ordinary and to acknowledge the mystery, and those who don't or won't.

(Michael Mayne, *This Sunrise of Wonder*, Fount, 1995, p. 16)

There was a time when Spanish coins had the Straits of Gibraltar on them with the words *Ne plus ultra*, meaning 'nothing beyond'. How things have changed; there is a whole New World beyond what was seen as the limits. The world has expanded in all directions, not only around the globe but into outer space and deep into the very make-up of our universe. We can view other galaxies and probe deep into the atom. Yet in a strange way people are often incapable of seeing beyond themselves or who they are.

Though we have extended our ability to communicate by telephone and the internet, we often fail to give our attention to what or who is in front of us. We can now see further into our universe than ever before, we can probe deeper into the very foundations of matter, but we fail to see what presents itself daily before our eyes. We fail to wonder at our own existence, our own being. St Augustine complained long ago:

> Men go abroad to wonder at the height of mountains, at the huge waves of the sea, at the long courses of rivers, at the vast compass of the ocean, at the circular motion of the stars; and they pass by themselves without wondering.
>
> (Augustine, *Confessions*, Book X, Chapter 8)

To live without wonder is to be undisturbed, unchallenged by the beyond in our midst. It is to have closed our eyes and our hearts to the mystery that is all about us, and to be untouched by the extraordinariness of our everyday world. The present is a gift waiting to be opened, yet most of us rush by to some future event without even noticing the wrappings. Enclosed in every moment and every encounter is the potential for wonder, for joy, for the gift of the Presence. If only we would open our eyes and give our attention, the world in which we live it is capable of suddenly showing us that we live in a wonderful environment. We can discover with Elizabeth Barrett Browning that:

> Earth's crammed with heaven,
> And every common bush afire with God:
> But only he who sees, takes off his shoes;
> The rest sit around it, and pluck blackberries,
> And daub their natural faces unaware
> More and more from the first similitude.
>
> (Elizabeth Barrett Browning,
> *Aurora Leigh*, Book 7, lines 82–6)

When it comes to retirement, there is a great opportunity to turn the mind and the heart to what really matters. You should have time to give your attention to yourself, your loved ones, the world around you, and to God. Of course there is the danger that you create a life as busy as before. Recently a friend who had just retired said that he had nothing to look forward to. Until now his life was measured by the agenda set for him, by the role he was asked to play and by how much he could get done in a period of time. It would seem he did not have a life of his own and that he found himself bad company. He had not learned to love himself or even listen to himself. He had been 'protected' from this by activity and being on the move.

Before we can reach out in confidence, or fully enjoy life we need to know ourselves, we need to love ourselves. If there is no love within, we cannot reach out in love. We need to know we are loved and to love our own being before we can have a love to share. Jesus recognized this when he said we are to love our neighbour as ourselves. Our neighbour often gets a hard deal because we are not comfortable with ourselves. We need to give attention to ourselves in wonder and awe and from that wonder and awe reach out. It is only by giving yourself time and value that you can know your own worth. You need to know that you are loved for who you are in your own uniqueness. It is a wonderful moment when you discover you are created out of the love of God and for his love. If you do not open your life to this awareness you may suffer from that great emptiness which only God can fill. Once we know we are loved we can reach out in love to others and know that the world around us offers us endless opportunities of giving ourselves in attention to others and to creation.

My friend failed to be aware of the joy of being and that each day offered wonder upon wonder. He could not contemplate the adventure of loving the great Other who is in our midst and so his days were empty. This is a sad comment on someone who has led an active life and is well educated. He had allowed his sense of encounter and wonder to atrophy, if it had ever been allowed to come fully alive.

This was described very forcibly by the Little Prince:

'I know a planet where there is a certain red-faced gentleman. He has never smelled a flower. He has never looked at a star. He has never loved anyone. He has never done anything in his life but add up figures. And all day he says over and over, just like you, "I am busy with matters of consequence!" that makes him swell with pride.'

'But he is not a man – he is a mushroom!'

'A what?'

'A mushroom!'

(Antoine de Saint-Exupéry, *The Little Prince*, Penguin, 1962, p. 31)

While I was on Holy Island, a pretty young woman opened the church door and said 'Is this Holy Island church?' When I turned to her and said, 'Yes, it is', her reply was 'Wow!' She stood at the door a couple of seconds and then left. She could say she had been. She could now go on and clock up the next place on her journey. I could not help but feel she was missing something.

There is a danger today of being forever on the move and just clocking up experiences and places. Tourist high spots are collected like collecting car number plates. There may be an occasional thrill but there is often little wonder that moves our whole being: if our senses are dulled nowhere will fill us with deep awe.

To keep their senses alert the Celtic races talked about playing the five-stringed harp, that is our five senses. As each sense has something to teach us of the world we have to keep them as healthy as we can. We have to use our senses and to be alert to what is around us. This is expressed rather quaintly by Thomas Traherne when he says, 'We need nothing but to open our eyes to be ravished like the Cherubims' (Thomas Traherne, *Centuries*, Faith Press, 1960, I, p. 37).

When dealing with the Scriptures the Celtic Church said that the New Testament needed the Old Testament so that we could understand it fully. The Old Testament in its turn needed the Primary Scriptures if we are to understand it. The Primary

Scriptures are the world and all that is in it. If we cannot read and relate to the world around us, it is hardly likely we will begin to understand its Creator. If our relationships with the world and with each other are not right we will not be able to have a good relationship with our God. It is through our awareness and openness to the world around us that wonder is able to enter our lives. Once we are aware of the wonder of life, of the existence of anything, we cannot treat it with disrespect or lightly. We begin to rejoice in its actual being, to become aware of its unique beauty. I believe much of this is captured in the traditional Jewish saying, 'On the Day of Judgement God will ask only one question: "Did you enjoy my world?" '

As those who believe in God the Creator, we should show that we love the world which our Father has given to us. We should delight in matter and in our humanity. Not only is this the world God has given to us, it is through it that God speaks to us and approaches us.

> All around us, to right and left, in front and behind, above and below, we have only to go a little beyond the frontier of sensible appearances in order to see the divine welling up and showing through . . . by means of all created things without exception, the divine assails us, penetrates us, moulds us. We imagined it as distant and inaccessible, whereas in fact we live steeped in its burning layers. *In eo vivimus.* As Jacob said, awakening from his dream, the world, this palpable world, which we were wont to treat with the boredom and disrespect with which we habitually regard places with no sacred association for us, is in truth a holy place, and we did not know it. *Venite adoremus.*
>
> (Teilhard de Chardin, *Le Milieu Divin*,
> Collins Fontana, 1964, p. 112)

Recently I was spreading a spoonful of honey on to my bread and became aware not only of the beautiful golden colour but the wonderful life of the bee. I reflected with sadness on how so many bees are endangered. To make a 500g jar of honey the bees that created it will have travelled as many miles as would have taken them around the world three times. When I take a single spoonful of honey I have before me the work that it took the lifetime of 12 bees to create. In this creation of 500g of honey, bees would have visited and helped to pollinate over three million flowers. This is precious stuff indeed. We ought to rejoice in the wonder of the creation of honey. The bread itself contains all the wonders of growth and co-operation. I often think upon these words when I take up my daily bread:

> Be gentle when you touch bread
> Let it not lie, uncared for,
> Unwanted.
> So often bread is taken for granted.
> There is such beauty in bread,
> Beauty of sun and soil
> Beauty of patient toil
> Wind and rain have caressed it
> Christ often blessed it
> Be gentle when you touch bread.
>   (Source unknown)

If only we would give our attention to what is around us our lives would be greatly enriched by what is offered to us at every moment. I have no doubt that the beyond is ever in our midst.

We cannot create wonder through words or by just seeing how things are made, though we can open our lives to the opportunity of wonder coming to us. The source of wonder and of joy is from the Other and is a gift from the Presence to which we respond in loving attention. The Other in its grace and goodness is willing to show us how extraordinary our world and our being are. But we will have to be open and responsive to this if we are to become aware and filled with wonder. Once again the Little Prince points us in the right direction:

'The men where you live,' said the little prince, 'raise five thousand roses in the same garden – and they do not find in it what they are looking for!'

'They do not find it,' I replied.

'And yet what they are looking for could be found in one single rose or a drop of water.'

'That is true,' I said.

And the little prince added: 'But the eyes are blind: one must look with the heart.'

> (Antoine de Saint-Exupéry, *The Little Prince*,
> Penguin, 1962, pp. 91–2)

Long before this St Augustine had said the same concerning seeing: 'Our whole business in this life is to restore to health the eyes of the heart whereby God may be seen.'

Wonder is not just about looking; it is about our whole being. It is only when we are willing to fully give ourselves, our time and our attention, that the Other will have room to give itself to us. This is true of people, of things and of God.

Wonder cannot be captured or tightly held; once we try to cling to it, it tends to disappear. It cannot be created on demand, though someone who is used to bowing before wonder can lead others to experience it for themselves. Once we begin to analyse wonder it means we have already lost it. The experience of wonder is approached with awe and is so often beyond all words. Wonder is the source of joy and it draws you out of yourself into a greater world, to the wonder of the beyond in our midst. Poets have often expressed the effects of wonder in their lives. Here is one of my favourites:

> I have felt
> A presence that disturbs me with the joy
> Of elevated thoughts: a sense sublime
> Of something far more deeply interfused,
> Whose dwelling is the light of setting suns,
> And the round ocean and the living air;

And the blue sky, and in the mind of man;
A motion and a spirit that impels
All thinking things, all objects of all thought
And rolls through all things.
> (William Wordsworth,
> 'Lines composed above Tintern Abbey')

Wonder comes often when we least expect it and with it comes a sense of awe and well-being. Even those who have hardened their lives can be suddenly touched or moved by an event or a person, by a piece of music or a work of art.

Just when we are safest, there's a sunset-touch,
A fancy from a flower-bell, some one's death,
A chorus-ending from Euripides, –
And that's enough for fifty hopes and fears,
As old and new at once as nature's self,
To rap and knock and enter in our soul.
> (Robert Browning,
> 'Bishop Blougram's apology')

My plea is to open your life to the wonder-full world. Let each day be a day of new awareness. For in opening your heart and eyes to what is about you, in being sensitive to what and who is around you, the hidden glory of God is able to enter into your life.

Thought

The one essential condition of human existence is that man should always be able to bow down to something infinitely great. If men are deprived of the infinitely great they will not go on living and die of despair. The Infinite and the Eternal are as essential for man as the little planet on which he dwells.
> (Fyodor M. Dostoyevsky, *The Possessed*,
> Modern Library, New York, 1963, pp. 674–5)

Exercise

Think over these words and seek to make them part of your daily experience.

Within each piece of creation,
within each person,
the hidden God waits
to cause us to laugh and surprise us with his glory.

Within each moment of time,
within each day and each hour
the hidden God approaches us
to call our name and to give us his joy.

Within each human heart,
within our innermost being
the hidden God touches us
to awaken us his love and his presence.

Everything is within him,
Space and time,
The human being and the heart.
God calls us to open our eyes
and our hearts to him and his will.

(David Adam, *Walking the Edges*,
SPCK, 2003, pp. 69–70)

O gracious and holy Father,
give us wisdom to perceive you,
intelligence to understand you,
diligence to seek you,
patience to wait for you,
eyes to behold you,
a heart to meditate upon you,
a life to proclaim you,
through the power of the Spirit
of our Lord Jesus Christ.

(St Benedict, *c*.480–*c*.550)